Advertising and the motor-car

Michael Frostick

Advertising and the motor-car

with a prologue by Ashley Havinden OBE, RDI, AGI

Lund Humphries · London

Copyright © 1970 Michael Frostick and Ashley Havinden

First edition 1970
Published by
Lund Humphries Publishers Limited
12 Bedford Square, London WC1

SBN 85331 242 7

Designed by Herbert Spencer and Hansje Oorthuys
Made and printed in Great Britain by
Lund Humphries, Bradford & London

Contents

Acknowledgments

No book of this scope is produced by one man – though he may finally write and assemble it. I would therefore take this opportunity to thank the many people who have been of assistance. Firstly Lord Montagu of Beaulieu, Michael Ware, and Eric Bellamy who through the medium of the Library at the Montagu Motor Museum did so much to provide many precious examples of early advertising without which the book could not exist.

My thanks are also due to many of the motor industry's Press Officers who, although acting in the course of duty, stretched themselves and their departments to the limit to be of help. I am also particularly grateful for the help of Alfred Woolf in London and Madame Rubiola and her staff in Turin who turned the Fiat Centro Storico upside down at my request.

Lastly I must thank Ashley Havinden for joining in so wild a project; and giving it a status it would not otherwise have.

Michael Frostick

Prologue by Ashley Havinden

Anyone who has tried to devote his career to the application of good design to advertising could hardly fail to be flattered – as I was – to be invited to write the prologue to this book by Michael Frostick. Not only has he earned his special niche in press and television motoring journalism – who has not admired his appearances on the BBC 2 TV programme *Wheelbase*? – but also he has shown a profound interest in and understanding of the problems of motor-car advertising.

Michael Frostick's idea of illustrating his history of the motor-car and its development over the years, not with pictures of cars and engines but with advertisements, is of especial interest because 'display' advertising as we know it today, as opposed to 'classified' and small 'reader' advertisements, began to emerge in the latter part of the nineteenth century – parallel with the birth of the motor-car. (See first illustration, on page 46, a Benz advertisement of 1888.) Thus the history of the one is 'enmeshed', as it were, to use a gear-box term, with the history of the other.

Just as the invention of the internal combustion engine soon led to the horseless carriage as a new form of transportation, so four other inventions in the field of communications during the nineteenth century produced an expansion of advertising techniques in the same period. Without these developments, many of the early (1888 onwards) posters, advertisements and catalogues reproduced in this book would never have existed. These four inventions were: lithography (1795–1862); photography (1834); the line-block (1872); the half-tone block (1882).

My association with Michael Frostick's book arises from the fact that I have been a car lover as well as being an advertising designer all my working life. And as Michael Frostick knew about this he approached me (as an advertising man) in August 1967 with the notion of my collaborating with him (as a motor-car man) in some way over the production of this book. This led us to a joint visit early in 1968 to the Motor Museum at Beaulieu. Our aim was not so much to see the great variety of actual motor-cars on view, but, in addition, as Michael Frostick had already arranged with his friend Lord Montagu, for us to have the much more important opportunity of studying the Montagu archives on the motor-car embodying the unique collection of ancient and modern advertisements, posters, booklets, and catalogues housed in special offices in Beaulieu Abbey. It was a fascinating experience for me; and after some hours, with various suggestions from Lord Montagu, who accompanied us for part of the time, we managed to make a selection of work to be reproduced: hence a great number of the illustrations in this book are from this invaluable source.

Naturally we discussed the book over dinner at Beaulieu; and, with its splendid variety of illustrations, the form it might take. Michael Frostick stressed '. . . the purpose of the book as being three-fold. That it is concerned with advertising and motor-cars is evident from the title, but equally important, though less evident, is the fact that it must be concerned with the sociological results of both the existence of personal transport and the effects that advertising have had upon it as a status symbol.' We agreed, of course, that this aspect was very important in terms of the quality of the design element in the appearance of motor-car advertising, particularly when one dwells on the great part the 'appearance' of the motor-car itself has played in its development towards social acceptance and the love of it as a 'beautiful object' which has been engendered in its adherents all over the world.

Michael Frostick continued his analysis of the structure of the book. 'All books concerned with the history of the motor-car fall readily into three historical divisions. Firstly, from its inception in the 1890's until the Great War (1914–18). Secondly, the period between the wars (1918–39), and, lastly, the period from 1945 to the present day. It is clear that the overall conception of this book must fall into these three divisions.' Michael Frostick agreed to undertake the arduous job of writing the main text; and I would add a general statement on the development of pictorial advertising techniques throughout the three periods. This statement could be illustrated by some of my own work in motor-car advertising as well as commenting in general on the illustrations appearing in the rest of the book which demonstrate the kind of advertising current throughout the three periods of motor-car development.

Although the history of 'modern' advertising could be said to start more or less at the same time as the history of the motor-car one must avoid the temptation to write a history of advertising: this would require a book all its own. One must accept therefore the limitation of commenting on advertising techniques as they developed, only in as far as they were, and are, expressed in motor-car advertising. This is a real limitation because a great deal of excellent work over this period was executed in 'product' fields other than the motor-car. Indeed, at this early stage, as was so often the case later on, the best creative effects in advertising, as far as the techniques of typography and illustration are concerned, unaccountably were not employed as much as they might have been in the field of the motor-car and its ancillary products.

For my part I find it more comfortable to express what I have to say about the whole subject of motor advertising in rather personal terms; and I hope the reader will bear with me in what may well look like an exercise in autobiography. Thus I will be able to explain how I came to benefit from some unusual influences early on in my career. This shaped my creative thinking and helped me to develop as an advertising designer in many fields, of which the motor-car was by no means the least important.

It all happened like this. In 1922, when I was 19, I joined as a trainee the firm of W.S.Crawford Ltd: forty-five years later I left it as Vice-Chairman. Crawfords was an advertising agency founded in London in 1914 by a Scotsman, William (later Sir William) Smith Crawford, who was head of the agency until his death in 1951. The year 1914 was unfortunate, to say the least, for the new agency since it was then that the First World War broke out; this gave it a very shaky start, since virtually all advertising ceased. It was not until 1920 that Crawfords began to make any progress under the leadership of William Crawford's dynamic and forceful personality. The war, of course, broke all sorts of long-established traditions and social conventions: more importantly, it also gave rise to a general ferment in the expression of new ideas in all fields of endeavour. A new page in history was turning over. Even politicians were promising 'a land fit for heroes to live in . . .' There was an urgent desire to start post-war life with a clean sheet.

I was extremely lucky to be entering a young advertising agency in the 1920's when the urgent new spirit of the age was affecting the creative fields of architecture, painting, the graphic arts, literature and, particularly, the printed word in new forms of typography and design.

The general appearance of 'advertising' just after the war was poor in terms of design and, as could be expected, still expressed the commonplace typography of the turn of the century period. This is shown in the advertisements reproduced in this book from the period 1888 to

1914 (pages 45 to 65). Unquestionably they are fascinating as museum
pieces, but with their amorphous muddle of unrelated elements, making
use of poor typefaces and often worse illustrations, they are obviously
the work of hacks. And, certainly, they had no aesthetic interest for me
in my early days at Crawfords. This period was too close in time, being
only twenty or so years in the past, and was sufficiently hateful to me to
generate the desire to get away from it at all costs. However, as we know,
'history is thirty years old', so the late nineteenth- and early twentieth-
century period (including *art nouveau*) is now old enough to be part of the
'ragbag' of the distant past which is tempting many young designers of
today to dip into it for 'new' ideas. I fear, therefore, that a lot of the
expression of this period may be coming back to masquerade as 'original'
solutions to present-day graphic problems. In my view, this is to be
deplored, because I don't believe the revival of such material will aid the
necessary constructive and creative attitude required in the latter part of
this increasingly technological century to solve the many problems involved in
all aspects of contemporary advertising design.

Before leaving this 'turn of the century' period, I might refer to two
examples illustrated in this book which show a little more sense of style
than the rest. First, the Argyll Motor Cars 1905 catalogue cover (page 57)
exhibits some self-conscious artistic pretensions in trying to produce a
unified design incorporating 'bulbous' lettering, the car itself and the
floating figure of Mercury, all carefully placed inside the not undistinguished
decorative border. This border is reminiscent of the later revival of
seventeenth-century 'printers' flowers' by Francis Meynell and Stanley
Morison in the 1920's printing renaissance, an echo of which is seen in
the 3-litre Bentley advertisement of 1925, on page 80, and the Rolls-Royce
Brewster of 1926, on page 85. Second, the 1913 Hispano-Suiza catalogue
illustration reproduced in colour on page 67. This is a charming
water-colour by René Vincent and is a good example of the break with
crude typefaces and indifferent illustrations which mar so much of
motor-car advertising in the early 1900's. It could be said to be among
the first examples of an artist's evocation of the joys of motoring which
we are to see again, for example, on page 82 in the 1924 Bentley colour
picture by Gordon Crosby.

At Crawfords in the early 1920's I was soon put in the studio on the 'layout' staff. This was most interesting, as it involved arranging all the elements in a given advertisement to fit the dimensions of the space 'booked' in the newspaper. This was usually 11 inches across 3 columns (6¾ inches wide in those days) because Crawford was keen on 'big' spaces. He could be said to have pioneered this size – and indeed, in the early 'thirties we worked mostly in 12 inches across 4 columns. This was a dominating size in a newspaper, and also had the advantage of being in proportion to the average full page in magazines – thus all that was required was a photographic reduction, if magazines were being used as well as newspapers. Sometimes we worked to 15 inches across 5 columns as well. A really big newspaper space!

Layout work involved deciding the size and style of lettering (or typeface) of the main headline, and co-ordinating this with the position and size of the illustration, together with the main text matter (copy), not forgetting the nameblock (usually a frightful piece of 'thickened-up script' based on the handwriting of the already defunct inventor of the product – and registered as a trade-mark in 1890!) which *had* to be displayed at the bottom of the advertisement. Frequently, the firm's 'slogan' also had to be displayed under the 'awful' nameblock.

These were the ingredients with which I wrestled in my early layout work in the Crawford studio in 1923. However, help and inspiration were at hand from totally unexpected sources.

Quite by chance an acquaintance of mine, G. H. Saxon Mills (who later became my best friend and working colleague at Crawfords until his death as a director of the firm in the late 'fifties), suggested we might get to know each other better if we dined in Soho one night. On the agreed evening Mills asked me to pick him up at his place of work in Westminster. I found that this was the small London office of the Curwen Press, where Mills was employed as secretary to Stanley Morison, who was allowed to use Harold Curwen's room, since Curwen was mostly at the printing works in Plaistow. However, on this occasion both Morison and Curwen, neither of whom I had ever heard of, were in the office – and I, a young man of 20, was introduced to these two men both nearly twice my age. Mills explained that I worked in an advertising agency.

Curwen was gracious and charming (I was to know him well later on as a distinguished printer, who did much to raise standards not only in the field of book production, but also in the many fields of jobbing printing for commercial undertakings in the 1920's – commissioning artists of the calibre of Claude Lovat Fraser and Edward Bawden to help him with illustrations and graphic embellishments). But Morison on the other hand pretended (very convincingly) to be outraged at the very idea of meeting me – pouring tremendous scorn on all advertising activities. Little did I realize then, that this dramatic (for me) encounter was to be one of the most significant moments in my life – altering my whole scale of values from then on. (I was soon to know Morison as a friend, for the rest of his life, until he died in 1967 – and also to appreciate that, even then, he was rapidly coming to be regarded as the greatest figure in the international field of typographical scholarship in this century.)

Morison's advice to me on this occasion was: get out of advertising and find something worth while to do – or, alternatively, *do* something constructive to improve the dreadful appearance of advertising (this is 1923) which was still reflecting the visual vulgarity of the late nineteenth-century printing and advertising with its crude illustrations, ugly display typefaces and even worse body types for the setting of text matter. Morison continued by observing that if I must work in advertising, I should try to do something like this – and at that point he handed me a small printed showcard he had on his desk for 'Eastmans' (the dry cleaners). This depicted a very 'cubist' sort of design in bright colours signed by an artist entirely strange to me: 'E Mc K K'. Morison went on to say that if I didn't like this, then I ought to get to like it, because it was an example of what the modern poster was going to be. Edward McKnight Kauffer was later to become famous for his 'Underground' and 'Shell' petrol posters among many others in the 'twenties and 'thirties. Ted Kauffer eventually became a great friend of mine and taught me a lot. I'm proud to say I persuaded Crawford to invite him to come to work for us on a full-time basis in 1927. Rather to my embarrassment, Crawford insisted, however, that although Kauffer was some ten years my senior, he would still have to work under me as his art director. Kauffer accepted this position with charming grace. One of the first jobs he did under my direction was the Chrysler car catalogue illustrated on pages 88 and 89.

After the 'Kauffer' shock was over, Morison then disclosed that in the previous year he had been appointed typographical adviser to the firm of

Lanston Monotype Ltd (later the Monotype Corporation) and handed me a beautiful little booklet (written and designed by him, and printed on hand-made paper at the Curwen Press) of the first showing of the Monotype 'Garamond' typeface (a re-cut version of the original Claude Garamond Roman and Italic types produced in Paris in 1540).

What a dichotomy: here was Morison stressing the latest form of outré poster designing and at the same time advancing the merits of a sixteenth-century typeface. The point seemed to be: modern painting for inspiration for poster design but a return to the past – well before the horrid late nineteenth-century period – for good typeface design and fine standards of book printing for inspiration in advertisement design in newspapers and magazines.

By the time Mills and I got to the Mars restaurant in Soho that evening I was in a state of agitation, a combination of pique and curiosity arising from this momentous experience at the Curwen offices, and particularly the confrontation with Morison. Who was he anyway? Mills then explained how important Harold Curwen, Stanley Morison, and others, like Francis Meynell of the Pelican Press, were in the twentieth-century typographical renaissance: and particularly Morison, who had, as an innovator and leading spirit at 'Monotype', made available to the printing trade (and advertisers) a whole range of marvellous classic typefaces from the sixteenth century onwards (Caslon, Garamond, Plantin, Poliphilus, Baskerville, Bodoni, Bembo, etc.) for use on the monotype casting machines. Mills went on to say that Morison had recently been appointed Typographic Adviser to the Cambridge University Press. Moreover, in spite of Morison's strictures on advertising, since 1920 he had himself been heavily engaged in it, though in a very special way, with Charles W. Hobson, a Manchester advertising agent and founder of the Cloister Press at Heaton Mersey, where he could produce fine printing for his clients.

The significance of Hobson in 1920 was that he sought to apply eighteenth-century culture to the look of his clients' advertising and printed matter. To this end he persuaded Haslam Mills (Mills's uncle) to leave *The Manchester Guardian*, where he had been leader writer, and to join him to write advertising copy; Morison similarly was persuaded to join as typographic designer. The result was a truly remarkable formula, quite different from any other advertising in the early 'twenties. This formula

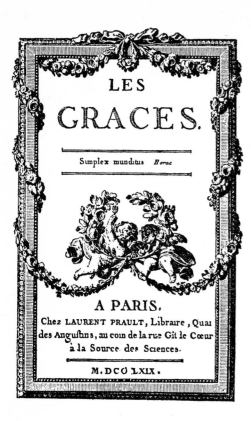

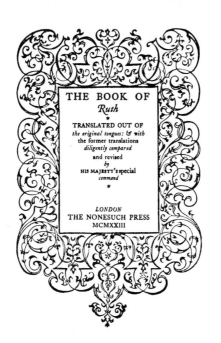

Old Friends to know. Old books to read. Old wood to burn. Old lawns to walk on. And let us add to this list of things that time improves—old shoes to wear.

But they must be shoes that had it in them to grow old. The Lotus Veldtschoen Shoes will be the possession of years. Watch them take the polish and, mingling the polish with the stains of grass and earth and weather, get the complexion of an old violin. A possession did we say? Yes, and a prize and pride as well

Lotus
VELDTSCHOEN
Boots: 63/-   Shoes: 55/- 60/-

LOTUS, LTD., STAFFORD & Northampton. *AGENTS EVERYWHERE*

THE NEW FLEETWOODS
The Ultimate in Luxurious Coachcraft

For those who desire a motor car expressing their own tastes and individuality, the Fleetwood Body Corporation has collaborated with the Cadillac Motor Car Company in interpreting in the new Fleetwood-Cadillacs and Fleetwood-La Salles the very ultimate in luxurious coachcraft.

Style—"the invariable mark of any master," individuality of appeal and perfect craftsmanship, these have long constituted an ideal and a tradition with Fleetwood. They are in very fact symbolized by the name Fleetwood.

Three generations of coach-crafters passed this ideal and this tradition to the present Fleetwood Body Corporation which has, since, uninterruptedly specialized in the production of custom-built bodies precisely interpreting owners' peculiar artistic perception and preference.

As in the days of Early American coachcraft, Fleetwood's successors to those Eighteenth Century artisans with their Old World traditions of craftsmanship, still produce the highest quality work, today specifically destined for those fields of motoring service where style factors—beauty, charm of contour, perfection of proportions, luxurious appointment—are paramount.

Representative creations of this famous line are now available in twenty-two exquisite models, Fleetwood designed and Fleetwood built, and can be had only in the new Cadillacs and La Salles. Varying body types and styles are on display in the Cadillac-La Salle showrooms of the more important centers throughout the country, and at our Salon and Studios, 10 East 57th Street, New York.

FLEETWOOD BODY CORPORATION
UNIT OF FISHER BODY CORPORATION · DIVISION OF GENERAL MOTORS

There is a woman so fastidious she has been known to spend hours dressing for a ball . . . so artistic she has furnished her home with rich treasures from the ends of the earth . . . so sagacious that she handles her own considerable financial affairs. She drives, or is driven in, a Rolls-Royce on every motoring occasion.

Only this best car, from every point of view, could please a nature so many-sided, so discriminating, as hers. The perfection of every last detail of her town car pays tribute to her costume and her destination. At the wheel of her roadster she delights when the silent motor whisks her over pike or country by-road with equal comfort, equal ease. Whenever she looks at one of her Rolls-Royce cars, she finds pleasure in the clean, distinguished lines—the proud cut of the bonnet which seems to welcome the road. And, though this consideration certainly comes last, she is glad to realize that her town car, purchased six years ago, is as satisfactory in appearance and performance as the roadster she bought this spring. She is convinced that serenity, superlative comfort and safety more than compensate for high initial cost! A one-hundred-mile trial trip will be arranged at your convenience. Rolls-Royce, Fifth Avenue at 56th Street, New York. Branches in principal cities.

ROLLS-ROYCE

Opposite, top left, an eighteenth-century title page by Moreau-le-Jeune, Paris, 1769. The eighteenth-century influence in the twentieth century is shown (top centre) by a title page by Francis (later Sir Francis) Meynell, Nonesuch Press, 1923; and top right by a press advertisement produced by C. W. Hobson Ltd in 1924.

Below are some examples of American motor-car advertising, demonstrating the Morison-Hobson (eighteenth-century) influence, c. 1926. Bottom left, Fleetwood Body Corporation advertisement with body type set in Monotype Cochin italics (Agents: T. S. MacManus Inc.). Bottom right, Rolls-Royce advertisement with a drawing by Rockwell Kent (Agents: N. W. Ayer & Son).

was: first, design a decorative border; next, arrange inside it, with ample white margins, a symmetrical composition (reminiscent of an eighteenth-century book title page) of the picture in wood-engraving style to match the beautiful printing types to be chosen by Morison to express Haslam Mills's terse and rhythmic prose in praise of the product; finally, design a 'nameblock' to match, and echo, the spirit of the illustration and the surrounding border. The result, of course, had classic grace and was wholly beautiful. Undoubtedly this formula raised the status, both in the trade, and in the eyes of the public, of Hobson's clients at the time (notably, Buoyant chairs, Lotus shoes, Meritor tooth-brushes, Dorcas fabrics, Robin Starch). Hobson had successfully persuaded them to admire design beauty and typographical distinction, so that their advertisements would stand out in contrast to the dreary commonplace announcements of their competitors – to their own great advantage!

It was the beginning, in advertising, of the typographical renaissance already taking place internationally in printing and publishing (in England: The Curwen Press, The Pelican Press, The Cambridge University Press and Francis Meynell's *Nonesuch* books; in America: the work and influence of admirers of Morison like D. B. Updike, Frederick W. Goudy and Bruce Rogers); and this was to make a huge impact on advertising and printing techniques in the 1920's.

I've dwelt at some length on this Morison episode in the early days of my career at Crawfords because of its far-reaching significance for my own work at the time and for advertising design in general. A number of examples (see pages 14 (Lotus, Fleetwood, Rolls-Royce), 34, 66, 79, 80 (Bentley), 85) demonstrate the classic style of symmetrically composed advertisements stemming from the Morison influence of the early 1920's.

Things began to move quickly after that Soho dinner in early 1923. Mills posted, within a day or two, some proofs of 'Hobson' advertisements. Armed with these I began to exhort my colleagues in the Crawford studio to produce work of comparable quality. As a mere junior trainee layout man, the presumption of my suggestions, implying criticism of their work, annoyed the studio manager so much that I was reported to Mr Crawford. He sent for me. In fear and trembling I went before him, with the Hobson proofs in hand, expecting to be fired, or at least severely reprimanded for insolence to my betters.

Crawford acted at once. He was fascinated by my urgent ideas. He had me moved from the studio, and for desk room, I was put into a small office with a young 'up-and-coming' account executive, Margaret Sangster (later to become my wife), and her secretary. There I was to be an independent layout man (with a biscuit tin to support my drawing board) to work out these 'Morison' layout and typographical ideas for any account executive who wished for them. Of course, my future wife immediately saw the practical advantages of getting me to work on her accounts, so saving the time often incurred in waiting for results from the main studio. Thus began a working partnership which lasted until she retired from Crawfords as a Director in 1962.

The next step was to get my friend Saxon Mills into Crawfords. Since he had left Morison he had edited *Commercial Art* and, then, the Imperial Airways house magazine. He was now mad keen to emulate his uncle Haslam Mills at Hobsons. I knew that he would be a copywriter sympathetic to my ideas; and that we could form, along with Margaret Sangster as account executive, critic, mediator and business manager, an integrated team which could produce a perfect blend of copy, layout and typography. Mr Crawford, to whom I had already introduced my mentor, Stanley Morison, and who saw the force of his typographical ideas, received my suggestion with enthusiasm. Saxon Mills, known to his family and friends as 'Bingy', was duly hired – incidentally at a higher salary than I was myself getting at that time! So was established, in late 1924, in a large room on the top floor of 233 High Holborn, the nucleus of a unique creative cell in the agency to serve existing clients specially selected by Mr Crawford as being most likely to respond to our ideas.

The clients were few to start with – but their number and importance began to grow. Of course, a lot of this could not have been done without William Crawford's constant encouragement and wise counsel; particularly valuable was his dynamic personality which convinced our clients and, what was perhaps more important, gave them confidence in the work we were doing for them.

During this period I was becoming quite a scholar of typography, spending most of my lunch hours in the British Museum studying the collection of rare books and manuscripts. Thus our main source of inspiration (as regards the appearance of the advertisements we contrived) was based on the work of printers and type designers from the fifteenth century onwards, which culminated in the refinement of all forms of artistic expression in the eighteenth century. The visual characteristics of that century can be summarised as follows: classical symmetry; a strong feeling for scale and proportion; gracious forms arranged to make balanced compositions; all elements in a design symmetrically disposed on each side of an imaginary centre line; and finally a vocabulary of formal decoration based on classical motifs and conventional arabesque floral patterns. This was the spirit of Georgian architecture; and it was echoed in all forms of expression in that period: furniture, silver, glass, textiles. It was also very much in evidence in printing layout and type design.

If typographical scholarship was the inspiration behind the work of Hobson and Crawford, it failed to find an echo in motor-car advertising in this country in the mid 'twenties. However, its influence was already permeating advertising design across the Atlantic. Fortunately for this book it found expression in a few motor-car advertisements produced in the USA. There are examples on pages 79 (Locomobile) and 85 (Rolls-Royce and Duesenberg) to which I shall refer later: and there is one for Fleetwood Bodies and another for Rolls-Royce illustrated in this prologue (page 14).

All this preoccupation with traditional typography which Bingy Mills shared with me, coupled with his ready wit and facility for writing good copy, with me doing all the layouts and the typography, as well as, frequently, executing the line drawings required for the illustrations, resulted with Margaret's help, in our producing, some fine work. Even Hobson tried to lure us away to his agency. However, such disloyalty to Crawford, who had so encouraged us, was out of the question. Also, our outlook was changing and indeed almost becoming 'anti-Hobson'! By the middle 'twenties we were increasingly less certain of the suitability as a solution to urgent twentieth-century problems of communication of what was indeed only a pastiche of the eighteenth-century printer's work. The classically symmetrical layout was becoming for us an inflexible straight jacket. After all, it was Hobson's special field anyway! Why should we not, therefore, try to explore entirely new avenues of advertising expression that could become uniquely 'Crawford' work?

This was an exciting new challenge for us in the mid 'twenties. The first clues as to how we might bring it about came from the continent. Quite by chance, in a bookshop in the Charing Cross Road, I found some

early Bauhaus books (1923–5 period) designed by Laszlo Moholy-Nagy.
He and his wife were later to become great friends of ours when he
moved to London in 1935. These books had the most extraordinarily
aggressive layout structure and typography, and extolled the new
'constructive' spirit in architecture, and especially in painting, following
the 'Dadaist' and 'Futurist' movements which emerged towards the end
of the First World War. This phenomenon was first expressed in 1921
in the paintings of Mondrian in Holland, El Lissitsky in Russia and
Moholy-Nagy in Germany; and, which was more important for me, it
was also carried over into the fields of printing and typography. The
principle of 'constructive' painting was based on the asymmetric balance
of forms in space. The principle of 'constructive' typography was the
application of this same asymmetry to the printed page in order to find
the freedom to rationalize all printed communication into its most
functional forms. The idea was that printed communication must be as direct
as possible: photographs should be used in preference to drawings, and
display types and text should be in block letters with no distracting serifs
or decorative flourishes. The picture and the text must be arranged
asymmetrically using the white space as part of the *dynamic* composition.

This could be a great development. It would allow much more scale
to the picture which, if necessary, could extend right to the edge of the
space. The text matter could be placed strategically in different parts of the
layout and in varying sizes according to the emphasis required. Such a
new form of typography was to be significant for its complete break with
the past, as represented by the traditional symmetrical arrangements of
classical typography, and, particularly, by the old typographer's love of an
'even colour' throughout the layout. The new 'constructive' typography
stressed the importance of emphasis through contrast, contrast of scale
and contrast of 'colour' by sudden changes in type sizes and weights.

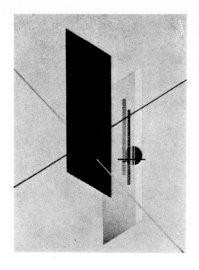

Examples of the 'asymmetric' principle. Opposite page, far left: Painting by Piet Mondrian, Holland, 1921; centre, Bauhaus title page by L. Moholy-Nagy, Germany, 1923; right, page from a booklet for NKF by Piet Zwart, Holland, 1923; above, painting by L. Moholy-Nagy, 1921.

Among the originators of 'constructive' typography at the Bauhaus were three now world-famous figures who, when they came to England in the mid-1930's, became personal friends of mine. These were, of course, Professor Moholy-Nagy, Professor Walter Gropius, and Herbert Bayer, who was one of Moholy-Nagy's most able pupils and is today an internationally known designer and painter working in the USA.

The Bauhaus was not alone in developing the idea of a new functionalism in typography. Influenced also by the experiments of the constructive painters, others were exploring the same possibilities in typography. El Lissitsky was himself trying it out in Russia, Piet Zwart in Holland (I managed to get hold of one of the now famous NKF cable catalogues which he designed in 1925, and which had a most inspirational effect on me) and Jan Tschichold in Switzerland. What was exciting about the 'new' typography, as it came to be called, was a conviction that the 'traditional' typographic approach to modern layout problems was outmoded – in the same way that the coming of the motor-car made the horse and carriage obsolete.

This was heady stuff for Bingy Mills, Margaret and me in the middle of the 1920's. We were already feeling the limitations of the symmetrical composition of illustration and text, one above the other; and particularly so in advertisement layouts and catalogue pages where dissociated elements had often required to be placed alongside each other in 'unbalanced arrangements' because the shape of the space available precluded the 'symmetrical'' superimposition of the elements. It will also be realized that the need for emphasis and the stressing of particular points, while rarely necessary in book typography, is really fundamental to advertising, if there is to be quick communication in the crowded space of newspapers and magazines. The advertising of the latest labour-saving products, moreover, requires a technique less redolent of the past and more in focus with the pattern of modern life, the life of the aeroplane, the motor-car, the candid camera and the moving picture.

On reflection, of course, looking back from today the whole process of the 'new typography' as related to advertising seems a logical and common-sense development; but at this time Bingy Mills, Margaret and I had only a vague understanding of what it was all about. As a designer, I had an 'intuitive' feeling of a new freedom to do remarkable things – a

great release from the bondage of the past. This generated a tremendous
excitement at the thought, untrammelled by tradition, of exploring
entirely new forms of layout and typographical ideas. The sky seemed
the limit: and a new client got the first impact.

In early 1925 the English agent for Chrysler cars decided to come to
Crawfords for his advertising.

Mr Crawford called us together and said that we now had a great
chance to do something really exciting. We all had trial runs in the Chrysler.
We were astonished at its terrific acceleration and flexibility in top gear.
These were entirely new qualities in American cars which had hitherto
the reputation in England of being big, cumbersome, and rather sluggish.
The only thing we didn't like about the car was its appearance. It seemed
tinny and unconvincing compared to the sort of cars we admired (we each
had a second-hand 3-litre Bentley at that time). We couldn't, of course,
tell our new client this. Naturally, he thought the car was beautiful and
wanted photographs of it to illustrate the advertisements. Bingy Mills,
Margaret and I had other ideas. We decided to put the whole emphasis
on *speed* and *performance* and to create advertisements which expressed this
as dramatically as possible. We proposed to use bold headlines (such as:
'Like an arrow along the wind – drive a Chrysler!') set at angles to the
horizontal. Sometimes I used straight lines of lettering, sometimes curved
ones, which I drew in heavy block letters with thin serifs applied to help

Illustrated on opposite page (greatly reduced) a newspaper half-page (also designed to be a double-page spread in magazines), and right, two newspaper spaces (also greatly reduced from 11 inches by 3 columns) showing examples of the first Chrysler campaign, 1925–7 period. The advertisement, far right, shows how well the style of the earlier hand-lettering of headlines has been translated by Monotype into a display typeface (*Ashley-Crawford*).

stress the direction of the lines, whether curved or straight. My lettering was later cut as a type at Morison's invitation by the Monotype Corporation under the name Ashley-Crawford. This was done in order to help the necessary proliferation of the advertisements in many languages which were to be required for use throughout Europe. Bingy Mills's short pithy copy I set in a well-leaded traditional 'seriffed' typeface (Monotype Plantin) for maximum legibility: for illustrations I used bold, and often extremely stylized drawings (many of which I executed myself), also placed at angles to suggest cars moving at speed across half-pages in newspapers, and double-page spreads in the motoring journals. We chose these large spaces (rare at the time) in order to announce this newcomer to the British car market in the most forceful possible way. The advertisements shown on this spread are typical of the campaign.

Our aim was to produce a new kind of dynamic effect which, with the major elements in the advertisement placed *at angles*, would *stand out* in the press by reason of bold 'contrast in weight' (i.e. degree of blackness) and, especially, by contrast to the normal appearance of the vertical columns, with horizontal text and headlines, in the rest of the pages, whether in newspapers or magazines. We also got rid of the 'nameblock' at the base, We felt the advertisement should be designed as a whole. The composition, like a constructivist painting, should be asymmetrically balanced in every detail, the bottom of the advertisement playing its part in the total composition just as much as the top, thus integrating the name of the product with the rest of the display.

This Chrysler advertising campaign of 1925 was the beginning of the new 'set-it-crooked' school of advertising design. So our detractors called it in the advertising journals of the time: we, of course, were delighted, regarding it as a great compliment to our work, to have produced any reaction at all. There can be no question, however, that at the time this new, bold and asymmetric approach to the designing of motor-car advertisements (echoing the original Bauhaus 'Moholy-Nagy' influence of 1923) was a landmark in British advertising. It was soon to be applied by us as a solution to other advertising problems for many different branded products with which we were concerned at that time. The expression of these new techniques rapidly became particularly identified with Crawfords as the new *modern* solution to the urgent problems of mid-and-late-'twenties advertising. It was thus that we finally broke away from the 'Hobson-Morison-eighteenth-century fixation' and so helped to establish Crawfords as the leading *modern* advertising agency.

Needless to say Mr Crawford was delighted with the proposals for our first Chrysler campaign. He soon helped us convince the client that this was the way to advertise the cars, because of their wonderful performance: also, that bold 'symbolic' drawings of the cars at speed were far more effective than static photographs, which, anyway, would not print well in the national newspapers; finally, that the basic aim of the advertising was not so much to 'sell' the appearance of the car, as to 'sell' its performance, and so get enquiries for trial runs and requests for catalogues. Aimed thus to arouse interest in 'owning-and-driving' a Chrysler, the catalogue was the proper place for photographs of the different models available, supported by the necessary explanatory text and detailed specifications.

The first half-page advertisements for Chrysler cars were launched with great effect in 1925. One of these, showing a layout which was used also in double-page spreads in motoring journals, I have reproduced here (very much reduced) on page 20. I have also shown on the same spread two '11 inches across 3 columns' advertisements (also reduced in proportion): the first, with running figures, is an announcement in 1926 for the Motor Show and the second is from a 1927 campaign showing the effect when the headlines are set in Monotype Ashley-Crawford. This demonstrates how well my hand-lettering for the earlier advertisements has been followed when translated into a typeface.

The success of the English advertising campaign of 1925–6 attracted the attention of the Chrysler Corporation in Detroit. The campaign had, in a short time, endowed the name 'Chrysler' with the aura of the most wanted cars in England. People were already beginning to talk, in the same breath, about 'Rolls-Royces, Bentleys, and Chryslers'. The Americans were so impressed that they decided to set up a plant in Antwerp, run by a forceful Detroit executive named Briggs, to assemble Chrysler cars for the European market. Mr Briggs called on Mr Crawford in London. They were roughly contemporaries, of the same stocky build and with similar ebullient personalities. They got on famously. Bingy Mills, Margaret and I were introduced to Mr Briggs, together with the head of Crawfords's fairly recently formed foreign department, Miss 'Peter' Hughes (later to be Lady Norton – the wife of the British Ambassador in Athens just after the Second World War, Sir Clifford Norton, KCMG). The result was that Crawfords were invited to take over all Chrysler advertising for Europe.

This was a big assignment, fraught with many practical difficulties. First, Mr Briggs, being an American, with experience only of a unified market in the States, wondered to what degree all the advertisements would have to be specially prepared in order to appeal successfully in twenty-two different languages and countries of Europe. This seemed a major problem until Mr Crawford produced a solution of elegant simplicity. His conviction was that the emotions of people the world over were basically the same, particularly when confronted with this new fascinating toy, the motor-car. After all, the car itself was to be the same in all markets and the appeal of its 'flashing' performance would be the same also. The style of the advertising and the drawings of cars at speed, therefore, would have the same universal appeal; only the words would have to be translated to suit the language of the different countries in which the car was to be marketed. Moreover, in Europe, as in England, the newspaper press with its poor printing – not suitable for half-tone photographs – was the best method of publicizing the cars.

Mr Briggs was fascinated by this conviction of Crawford's, and so Miss Hughes (a great personality and well-known to the European press) was instructed to visit all the countries concerned and to try, as Crawfords's representative, to organize on behalf of the Chrysler Corporation the booking of newspaper spaces approximating to the sizes used in England. Thus the dramatic English advertisements could be syndicated throughout Europe without loss of impact. The only problem would be to arrange for the translation of the headlines and text into the appropriate languages. The headlines, to be set in Ashley-Crawford, presented no typographical problems as the Monotype Corporation was able to make this particular typeface available in most European countries. The whole conception took some organization; but it had many advantages never before exploited. Suggestion, rumour, excitement and the simple dramatic appeal, in straightforward language, to the 'international human being', made it possible for the basic Chrysler advertising campaigns to succeed in every country with equal effect despite differences of national temperament.

By 1927 a new inspiration came into our lives in the form of a fascinating book, *Towards a new architecture*, by Le Corbusier, which had been translated from the French by Frederick W. Etchells. By 1929, this led Mr Crawford to invite Etchells, whom we had all met as a friend of Ted Kauffer, to redesign, and practically rebuild, the entire structure of the Crawford building at 233 High Holborn, where the agency still operates today (now a scheduled building of historic importance). Le Corbusier's brilliant exposition of the necessity not only for modern architecture, but also for modern design in all fields of man's ingenuity ('. . . a house is a machine for living in'), including motor-cars, made a huge impact on us.

The stimulation of Le Corbusier's book, which expressed in such convincing and colourful language much the same philosophies of design which the Bauhaus under the leadership of another architect, Professor Walter Gropius, had been pursuing since 1921, led us by 1927 to a greater study and understanding of the principles of the new typography as expounded in the writings of Moholy-Nagy and, above all, by Jan Tschichold. Ideas of this kind were to find expression in our later work for Chrysler.

My early zest for dynamic expression for its own sake – in order to break away from a preoccupation with traditional symmetrical typography as a solution to advertising layout problems – thus gradually gave way to a more ordered approach, as the principles of rationalism and functionalism in the new continental typography were increasingly understood by us in Crawfords. Our fresh thinking was to be expressed in an entirely new campaign for Chrysler cars.

It was clear by 1928 that the scale of Chrysler's operations in Europe demanded an original and more flexible campaign. Mr Briggs called a meeting in Antwerp, which Mr Crawford, Peter Hughes, Margaret, Bingy Mills and I all attended, to discuss future work. We appreciated that the growing advertising requirements in many media (newspapers, magazines, posters and display material for dealers' showrooms, leaflets and catalogues) demanded some unifying motif. This must be different and distinct from the general 'dynamism of headlines at angles' and bold drawings of cars rushing about newspaper spaces, which had been the basis of the advertising since Chrysler started in Europe.

We returned to London and immediately set to work. The outcome was the creation of what came to be known as the 'dream car' campaign. Each advertisement, or manifestation according to the media requirement, was like 'a chapter in an endless novel'. Each was the same and yet different. The whole campaign 'had legs' (as Margaret used to say of a campaign of any quality). It was unified throughout by the creation of a unique design motif, namely the extremely stylized and geometrically drawn (by me) symbol of a car conveying the impression of great 'smoothness' at speed. We decided to drop the Monotype Ashley-Crawford type for the display of headlines, choosing a simpler more functional sans-serif letter which was readily available throughout Europe in a range of sizes, Erbar Bold (designed by J. Erbar and produced by the German typefounders Ludwig & Mayer in Frankfurt-on-Main); but we retained for text matter an efficient legible reading type such as the traditional Monotype Plantin which we had used since the inception of our Chrysler advertising.

The 'dream car' campaign was great fun to carry out. Some of its requirements were 'adapted' in the Crawford Paris and Berlin offices for more rapid servicing. The bulk of the work, of course, was in black and white for newspaper reproduction, but a number of opportunities arose to use colour for catalogues, posters and display material. A few examples of this campaign are fairly fully illustrated in this prologue to show the

MORE POWER FROM YOUR

PETROL

Motorists demanding higher and still higher efficiency from their engines—

Yet ordinary petrol would not work properly in a high compression engine—

That was the problem Chrysler faced.

That was the problem Chrysler solved with his wonderful Silver Dome engine.

The Silver Dome engine gives the power of a high-compression engine—

Yet it runs smoothly and silently on ordinary petrol.

It has a specially shaped cylinder head. And when ordinary petrol vapour enters the cylinders the Silver Dome head sets the gas whirling inside the cylinder. Then the spark! The spinning gas burns evenly, quickly, thoroughly, giving out its full power. Making your Chrysler soar up the longest hill. Giving you vivid acceleration for easy driving in traffic.

CHRYSLER!

Three great 6-cylinder ranges—Chrysler Imperial 80, from £940; Chrysler 75, from £515; Chrysler 65 from £375. Chrysler cars of every type and price. See the models in the dealer's showrooms. Write for catalogues

CHRYSLER MOTORS LTD · KEW GARDENS · SURREY

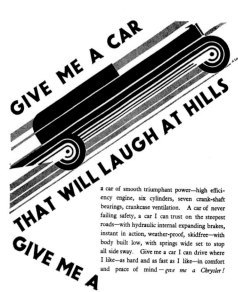

GIVE ME A CAR THAT WILL LAUGH AT HILLS GIVE ME A

a car of smooth triumphant power—high efficiency engine, six cylinders, seven crank-shaft bearings, crankcase ventilation. A car of never failing safety, a car I can trust on the steepest roads—with hydraulic internal expanding brakes, instant in action, weather-proof, skidfree—with body built low, with springs wide set to stop all side sway. Give me a car I can drive where I like—as hard and as fast as I like—in comfort and peace of mind—*give me a Chrysler!*

CHRYSLER!

Three great 6-cylinder ranges—Chrysler Imperial 80 from £940, Chrysler 75 from £515, Chrysler 65 from £375! Chrysler cars of every type and price. See all the models in the dealer's showrooms.

WRITE FOR CATALOGUES · CHRYSLER MOTORS LTD · KEW GARDENS · SURREY

The four greatly reduced advertisements, left, are massed together to show at a glance what is meant by a campaign. Although these are only a fraction of the number of 'dream car' advertisements produced from 1928 onwards for use throughout the UK and Europe, they demonstrate the visual variety (and 'follow through') that can be achieved on a single theme. Like 'a chapter in an endless novel', each is the same and yet different. Opposite is a full page (slightly reduced from the original size) showing an advertisement in Spanish, which is typical of how well the campaign 'adapted' for Europe into over twenty different languages, whilst still retaining the basic visual theme (Agents: W.S.Crawford Ltd).

SEE–SEE

CHRYSLER 65!

Her speed—sixty-five miles an hour and more. Her engine—'Silver Dome' high efficiency—six cylinders, counterweighted seven-bearing crankshaft. Her brakes —hydraulic internal-expanding—skidfree, weather-proof, light acting! How beautiful she looks now as she flashes by! The new slender radiator, the low harmonious curves of bodywork and wings—fascinating, satisfying —setting a new ideal in motor car beauty. Isn't that the car for you? *And for me!* See the Chrysler 65 in the dealers' showrooms to-day! Try one out on the road!

Three great 6-cylinder ranges—Chrysler 65 from £375, Chrysler 75 from £515, Chrysler Imperial 80 from £940. Chrysler cars of every type and price. See the models in the dealers' showrooms to-day

WRITE FOR CATALOGUES · CHRYSLER MOTORS LTD · KEW GARDENS · SURREY

WHEN STREETS ARE WET AND CROWDED —

GIVE ME A

give me a car with smooth lightning pick-up—six cylinders, seven crankshaft bearings—to flash away from traffic blocks in top gear. Give me hydraulic internal-expanding brakes—never-failing, non-skidding even when used suddenly on greasy roads. A car built low for steadiness, with wide clear windows, controls which are simple, light-acting, just where I want them. Give me a—

CHRYSLER!

Three great 6-cylinder ranges—Chrysler Imperial 80 from £940, Chrysler 75 from £515, Chrysler 65 from £375. Chrysler cars of every type and price. See the models in the dealers' showrooms.

WRITE FOR CATALOGUES · CHRYSLER MOTORS LTD · KEW GARDENS · SURREY

AHORA ¡EL

PLYMOUTH!

Su carroceria—de lineas suaves y armoniosas, asientos amplios y profundos—es tan lujosa como bella.

Su motor—"Silver Dome," cuatro cilindros y de gran rendimiento, alcanza velocidades de 65—80—100 kilómetros por hora con perfecta suavidad.

Sus frenos—hidráulicos, de expansión interna y acción instantánea, ofrecen absoluta seguridad a cualquier velocidad, en cualquier carretera, lo mismo en tiempo húmedo que seco.

Que otro coche hay tan amplio, rápido y silencioso por precio tan moderado?

Existe otro coche tan fácil de conducir?

El representante del Plymouth está dispuesto a darle una demonstración cuando Vd. guste.

EL ULTIMO EXITO DE CHRYSLER

AGENCIA EXCLUSIVA PARA ESPAÑA: S.E.I.D.A. (S.A.), FERNANFLOR NÚM 2, PISO I°, MADRID
VENTA AL PÚBLICO: AVENIDA DE PI Y MARGALL 14
Chrysler Sales Corporation, Detroit, U.S.A.

variety that can be achieved in appearance on the same theme (pages 26 and 27); also in the body of the book on pages 88 and 89 (a catalogue) and pages 90 and 91 (two press advertisements).

I've written at some length about the Crawford-Chrysler story because Michael Frostick said he'd always regarded it as significant, if not unique, in the history of motor-car advertising. In fact one of the main reasons why he suggested I should be involved in this book was so that I would give some of the details, and the background history, of this one motor-car manufacturer who succeeded in mounting for a number of years a co-ordinated advertising campaign with a uniquely integrated design policy throughout Europe.

Unfortunately the history of this particular work was concluded, more or less, at the beginning of the 'thirties. The great slump in America, which began in the early 'thirties, led to Mr Briggs being recalled to Detroit and our Berlin office being closed soon after. The situation was becoming extremely difficult for the principal reason that Chrysler had always collected the total annual advertising revenue in various proportions from their main dealers throughout Europe. Chrysler then forwarded these moneys to Crawfords, who, as their advertising agent, was responsible for paying the newspapers, printers and other suppliers. Chrysler were in a strong position to collect this money, since they could always threaten dealers with cutting off the supply of cars if they would not pay promptly their agreed proportion of the advertising appropriation. However, Chrysler now insisted that Crawfords in future must collect this money from each of the Chrysler dealers. Mr Crawford immediately foresaw the difficulties, from an administrative point of view, of doing this, but, more seriously, he envisaged the financial risk involved. The agency could easily be burdened with numbers of bad debts, since Crawfords obviously would not be in the same strong bargaining position *vis-a-vis* Chrysler dealers as the car manufacturers. Reluctantly, therefore, Mr Crawford decided that he had no alternative but to give up the account. This decision, with which we agreed as Directors of Crawfords (Margaret, Bingy Mills and I were all put on the Crawford Board together in 1929), was a sad one. Chrysler was not only one of our biggest accounts but was also the main reason for our operating in Europe, chiefly from the Berlin office. Although we had a number of other European accounts, mostly German domestic products, which were run from the German office, the loss of Chrysler revenue coupled with the potential rise of Hitler forced the inevitable decision to close our very smart and modern Berlin establishment.

It is perhaps sad when one thinks of the way in which Crawfords had produced a unique and distinguished corporate image for Chrysler cars throughout Europe for some six or seven years, to see top centre on page 100 of this book the Chrysler advertisement of 1938 which clearly has *not* got the Crawford touch. (Chrysler, with new management, had come back into the English market and chosen another advertising agent.) Without any distinguishing features it merges in with all the other advertisements on page 100. I am reminded of one of Sir William Crawford's great principles: 'continuity'; and I recall also his conviction that 'domination, concentration and repetition' were essential to build up both knowledge and respect for a product. This was the basis of all successful advertising. When the public is so bombarded with advertising in a plethora of forms, how can a product 'emerge' and become a *public favourite*?

Another of Sir William Crawford's principles of advertising was (like golf) the importance of 'follow through'. Finding a 'theme' is the first problem; but, once found, *stick to it*. It takes at least two to three years to get public recognition. Once won there is no reason why a successful campaign theme should not run for decades. It is useless to exploit a dramatic theme for only twelve months or so and then throw it away. Why . . . ? Perhaps the most consistent advertising policy of recent times in the motor-car field has been the sustained campaign for Volkswagen. Its clever theme (evolved by the American agency Doyle, Dane & Bernbach) has been going now for some years and it still continues just as successfully.

Alas! Today – as in the 'thirties – there is still too much chop-and-change.

I think it was the late Wells Coates, the great architect, who once said to me: 'the problem for creative people is not so much the ability to do good work, but the ability to create the conditions in which it can be done.' Sir William Crawford was rare, as an employer, because he had an instinctive understanding of the value of such a dictum. It is because of this that Margaret, Bingy Mills and I had so much scope to express our creative convictions in Crawfords. He supported fully the great lesson I first learnt from Stanley

Morison in 1923: not to be supine in accepting what other people say, but to be arrogant enough and to try to be knowledgeable enough to have the confidence to challenge everything in the belief that there must be a better, more inspired solution to current problems than the banal and the obvious. As Bingy Mills loved to repeat: 'There are far too many people already keeping the world safe for mediocrity!' Certainly, we had the zest under Bill Crawford's leadership to attempt the unusual in all our activities; and sometimes it even proved to be the impossible.

Our links with advertising in the motoring field became relatively tenuous after the great preoccupation with Chrysler for so many years. We did produce, however, a campaign of advertisements for 'India tyres' in the early 'thirties, which was based on the graphic conception of tyres rolling across newspaper spaces (11 inches across 3 columns) spelling out displayed words in ribbon-like form. A fairly typical example (greatly reduced) is the single advertisement illustrated on this page. In the same period (1931–33) we had some fun doing a series of dynamic campaigns for BP petrol with symbolic cars (slightly reminiscent of Chrysler – only this time I executed them with the air-brush in place of the pen) rushing about newspaper spaces (11 inches across 3 columns). Two of this series of advertisements (also greatly reduced) I have shown on the opposite page as examples of the variety of appearance that can be achieved in a campaign based on the same theme.

We also did a major campaign for 'Motorine oil' in the early 'thirties in large spaces (12 inches across 4 columns). The theme was to link 'Motorine' with the names and photographs of all the many makes of cars whose manufacturers specifically recommended this oil as the best for their engines. Of course, a great feather in Motorine's cap was the support of Rolls-Royce for over twenty years. The layout structure, in this case a device for holding the top to the bottom of each advertisement in the campaign, was the idea of linking the two o's in MOTORINE by parallel lines (sometimes vertical, sometimes at an angle) passing through the text to the word OIL at the base of the advertisement. To illustrate this campaign I've chosen two examples from opposite ends of the spectrum of motor-car ownership: the classical architectonic expression of the stately Rolls – a very formal layout – to the more spritely layout of the little Singer saloon. These are shown together on pages 32 and 33.

Three advertisements (all greatly reduced) showing on opposite page one example of the 1931 India Tyre campaign; and, right, two examples of the 'BP' petrol campaign of the same period (Agents: W.S.Crawford Ltd).

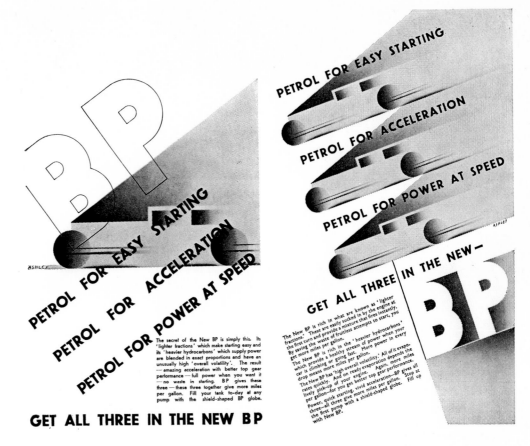

After the outbreak of the last war in 1939 many motor manufacturers in order to keep their name alive began to resort to 'prestige' advertising (as it came to be called), because obviously they would have few cars to sell. The Ford Motor Company came to Crawfords at this time. For this 'big' company we designed a campaign requiring 'big' spaces, full pages in magazines and 12 inches across 4 columns in newspapers. We produced a great number of advertisements, the general theme of which was to play on various aspects of the war effort with a base line 'so – FORD MARCHES ON . . .' I've chosen as an illustration here (page 34) one which appeared in 1940, which I think is rather impressive. Bingy Mills (who wrote the copy) agreed with me that a symmetrical layout would be the most dignified presentation for these Ford announcements. So I had the body type set in a well-leaded classic Monotype face, and the headlines in Times Bold capitals, the whole surmounted with scraper board drawings of great distinction executed under my direction by Collett, a free-lance artist whose work we admired.

So much for my own connexion with motor advertising. As one who has devoted nearly half a century to the profession of designing for industry and commerce, I appreciate that I run the risk of overstaying my welcome in this prologue: I will, therefore, confine myself to commenting on just a few of the – to me – more interesting advertisements from the international field which Michael Frostick has selected for us in the main body of this book.

MOTORINE

Magic genius of Rolls-Royce that has given to so much power such silence and such silken sweetness! Magic quality of Motorine, that adds still greater smoothness to this smoothest of all cars! With all the oils of the world to choose from, Rolls-Royce have used Price's Motorine for over twenty years. How then can you run **your car** on any oil but this — with Motorine available for every car on the road — with Motorine costing no more than other oils? Use Motorine — always!

 **OIL**

PRICE'S LONDON SW 11

The two illustrations on this spread (both reduced from 12 inches by 4 columns size) show typical examples of newspaper advertisements from the 'Motorine Oil' campaign of the early thirties (Agents: W.S.Crawford Ltd)

MOTORINE

Listen to the merry hum of Singers speeding past! There's a lively engine! How to keep it smooth and sweet year after year? How else but with Price's Motorine — recommended by Singer for the last six years? Motorine — refined from the pick of the world's raw oils. Motorine — used by Rolls-Royce for over twenty years. **Price's Motorine — costing no more than other oils.** Use the grade blended to suit your car.

OIL

PRICE'S LONDON SW11

I think the 1916 Locomobile catalogue cover and inside pages (shown on page 79) is a beautiful piece of American design. It has the authority of the classical approach in its layouts and typography which impart a feeling of cleanliness, efficiency and great quality to the car.

On page 85 there is a charming American advertisement of 1926 for Rolls-Royce Brewster (produced by Young & Rubicam). This has all the eighteenth-century qualities of beautiful symmetry and loving typography. It couldn't have been better if designed by Stanley Morison himself. Also the 'Duesenberg' of 1929, alongside, is a very good American example of symmetrical typography in a simple, if rather plain, announcement.

To change the tempo from the 'classical' approach to the 'modern', the two catalogue covers on page 93 are interesting. The top picture, for the Italian Issota Fraschini (IF) of 1933, is well designed and curiously reminiscent of the Chrysler 'dream car' work we did in 1930–1! The

BUT MOTORING MUST GO ON!

War cuts a rift across the lives of all of us. Habits change—almost overnight. New conditions swirl up—settle down upon us.

But *motoring* must go on. The Government wishes that. The nation's business demands it.

So Ford—ever marching on—brings to you the new wartime car—the "Anglia," the latest triumph of Ford engineering.

It is built to give exceptional mileage on 'pool' petrol. It has the all-round economy and modest tax of an efficient 8 h.p. car. It meets the needs of everybody these days.

Yet—see what brilliant Ford engineering has combined with these ! Impressive appear-ance. Lively performance. Spacious interior. The large outside luggage compartment and generous equipment.

.   .   .

A car produced for wartime—and a car which would make its mark in the easy days of peace ! . . .

From the great Ford factory at Dagenham by the Thames large numbers of the "Anglia" are now streaming forth. The Ford dealer in your neighbourhood has one to show you.

See it. Try the "Anglia" ! You *need* this new car for the new times. Britain asks for such a car.

SO...FORD MARCHES ON...

Prologue by Ashley Havinden

bottom picture for the French Delahaye of 1938 is very stylish and much influenced by modern art of the day in its execution. Also from 1938 there is an excellent German catalogue cover and inside pages for Mercedes. This is shown on a double-page spread (pages 102 and 103) and illustrates the high standard of artwork and typography in a straightforward idiom that we have associated with Mercedes's work over many years.

The latter part of the book, before the final section *Seventy years of Fiat advertising*, is filled with a great number of lush advertisements, many in colour, which the reader will recognize as typical of the usual American approach to the advertising of their luxury cars for 'men of distinction'. The production technique and quality of the 'artwork' is mostly of a high order.

The final section of the book, devoted to the Italian Fiat advertising from 1899 to 1969, is fascinating by presenting the history, in all its strange advertising phases, of *one* motor-car from its inception to the present day. There is much of interest in this section where one is given the opportunity to trace the various changes that have taken place, from the run-of-the-mill commonplace work done at the turn of the century, right up to all forms of 'ultra modern' expression.

The reader will by now want to get on with the book. It occurs to me that if he has followed me thus far, I might assume from what he has read, that his own critical faculties and appreciation of advertising design – if they weren't before – are now sufficiently acute to be able to form his own judgements. This book, after all, is meant not only to show the best of motor-car advertising, which is rare enough, but also to give a broad picture of the *typical* as seen by the public over some seven decades. The reader therefore will be sensitive to the wheat as well as to the chaff in his assessment of both the design qualities and the social significance of the advertisements chosen by Michael Frostick to illustrate his unique study of the motor-car from its inception in the late 'nineties to the present day. I wish it well.

Birth pangs: 1885-1914

'That day no common task his labour claim'd:
Full twenty tripods for his hall he framed,
That, placed on living wheels of massy gold,
(Wondrous to tell) instinct with spirit roll'd
From place to place, around the blest abodes,
Self-moved, obedient to the beck of gods.'
HOMER. *Iliad* Book XVIII
(Pope's translation)

The trouble with the motor-car, from an historical point of view, is that no one person seems to have invented it and no date can be put upon its birth. Unlike the telephone, which Hollywood is happy to attribute to Don Ameche, or television, which fairly clearly belongs to Baird (even though he was using the wrong system), the motor-car belongs to no one. Much the same might be said of advertising; for who can say when the first advertisement was written? Who knows what words, upon what wall, first bade the onlookers to come and buy? All we can say is that the Town Crier might usefully be regarded as the precursor of the Radio Commercial.

When considering vehicles we must be careful in our choice of words, for the use of the term 'motor-car' clearly implies an internal combustion engine driven by petrol, or perhaps *in extremis* by gas. In the early days then, it is perhaps better to choose the more usual American term of 'automobile' which, although nowadays implying propulsion by means of internal combustion, can more happily be used to describe any self-propelled vehicle. From this springboard we can go back to the Iliad where we find, in a reference to a visit to Vulcan's forge, the lines quoted above.

Taking a cynical twentieth-century view, it is probably safe to assume that Homer's vehicles did not in fact exist; and were only the precursors of many similar ideas which got no farther than the drawing board. However, it is recorded that in 1479 the city of Antwerp purchased for the sum of twenty-five livres from one Gillies de Dome, a mechanically propelled vehicle; but even here we may fairly safely assume that it was mechanically propelled rather than mechanically powered. In 1600 Prince Maurice of Nassau had built for himself by one Simon Stevin a land yacht which he used on the beach near Scheveningen – this was supposed to have carried twenty-eight frightened Dutchmen at speeds as high as fifteen miles an hour; but in all these things we are in fact in cloud-cuckoo-land.

We come down to earth with a bump, however, in 1769 when Nicolas Joseph Cugnot, a French Army engineer, built a gun tractor powered by steam. This vehicle, which still exists in the Conservatoire Nationale des Arts et Métiers in Paris and models of which are to be found in both London and Turin, was really the father of the automobile. It was a three-wheeler with a chassis built of heavy timbers and a great pear-shaped copper boiler in front of the front wheel. Two massive cylinders poised on either side of this same front wheel drove it forward, at something like six kilometres an hour. And though it had to stop every fifteen minutes to boil more water there is little doubt that Cugnot was the first man to sit behind the wheel of a self-propelled vehicle. It might also be regarded as a powerful argument for having the engine in front driving the front wheels. Sadly, however, Cugnot's mechanical knowledge was better than his understanding of the science of road holding, for with this immense weight driving the front wheels the vehicle left the road out of control and plunged into a ditch, there to end its own life ignominiously in giving birth to the motor-car.

With the coming of the railways and the widespread use of steam power in industry, it was natural enough that Cugnot's gun tractor should be followed by a wide variety of steam vehicles. In 1784 Murdoch, a Cornishman from Redruth, built a small three-wheeled model which carried no persons and which ran away from him one dark night, earning itself the right to be regarded as the first self-powered vehicle to terrify a pedestrian, for it is recorded that the village parson who saw it in flight thought Beelzebub was abroad on the roads! Trevethick, another famous engineer of the time, built a machine which could carry eight people 'faster than a man could walk', and in the United States in 1805 Oliver Evans, of Newport, Delaware, built an amphibious steam-powered dredge called the 'Orukter Amphibolus' which, according to contemporary description, waddled through the streets of Philadelphia into the Schuylkill river under its own power.

From then on men everywhere were building steam vehicles: in Halifax, Nova Scotia, in Prague, and in Hartford, Connecticut, and more particularly in England where there was a boom in road locomotives.

From about 1820 onwards, after Telford and Macadam had greatly improved the road system, a number of steam coaches operated regularly in place of the horse-drawn variety; and together with these, steam tricycles and steam buggies abounded. They provided, for a limited number of people, a successful form of transport and, for the cartoonists of the day, endless delight; but as is so often the case with new developments their blossoming was shortlived. In 1831 a committee reported to the Houses of Parliament in favour of steam coaches and a reduction of the road tolls, but the powerful forces against steam finally won and by 1840 the steam carriage had almost disappeared from the King's Highway. To what extent these steam behemoths had affected the life of the everyday man is far from certain. Communication then was not what it is now; and unless a steam bus ran past your door it was probably of little interest. However, the awakenings of the Industrial Revolution had begun to make people conscious of the possible developments, and at least at exhibitions the world in general was made aware of the existence of steam vehicles and advertising began to play its part.

When it comes to the motor-car the situation is, if anything, even more obscure. For general purposes it may be accepted that Benz and Daimler working separately in about 1885 produced the first motor-cars as we understand them. The other two claimants are the Frenchman Etienne Lenoir and the Austrian Siegfried Marcus. Many claim that Lenoir was really the father of the motor-car, and as early as May 1862 he is reputed to have built a horseless carriage which ran several times between Paris and Joinville-le-Pont. The kind of fuel he used seems to be somewhat in doubt, but one thing is quite certain and that is that he was the father of the internal combustion engine in France. As for Siegfried Marcus, he built two cars in the 1860's and 1870's and his claim is strengthened by the fact that one of the cars not only exists in the Vienna Museum but can still be driven. The first British vehicle seems to have been Butler's Tricycle in which he went to great lengths to avoid infringing the four-cycle patents of Doctor Otto. This question of patents was one which was to bedevil the industry in its early years, reaching its peak in the famous Seldon case in which Henry Ford fought for the entire motor industry and eventually won.

From this point onwards we have motor-cars and in no time at all we have a motor industry. Given an industry we have salesmen, and given salesmen we have advertising. The development of the motor-car was slower in England than it was in the rest of the world due to the prohibitive legislation which was introduced. There were, in fact, four Locomotive Acts. Of these, three, one in 1861, another in 1865, and another in 1878, as well as a portion of the Local Government Act of 1888, were devoted to the locomotive. A locomotive was held to mean in law any vehicle propelled by any power except animal (which presumably included the human race!). Before 1896, if anybody wished to use a motor-car or, as we should say in law, a locomotive, at least three men had to be employed to drive it and also a man to walk in front, the earlier Acts having decreed that he should carry a red flag. He must observe a three mile an hour speed limit and pay a licence fee of £10 for each county through which he drove. He was further restrained from crossing any bridge unless it bore a notice permitting him so to do. These restrictive regulations were swept away by the fourth Locomotive Act of 1896, which at least allowed the maximum speed to be raised to 12 m.p.h., but before this last Act and as a result of the previous laws there was virtually no British motor industry at all.

Both the French and the Germans were already turning out cars and motor-cycles in quite large numbers, and in America the Duryea brothers and others had set up as manufacturers even if they were not really producing in any great numbers. The British industry therefore began not as manufacturers but as tradesmen and car salesmen, and H. J. Lawson, a colourful character, is frequently regarded as the father of the British motor industry because he set up a large business for importing motor-cars. In 1895 this gentleman formed the British Motor Syndicate. This 'Syndicate' not only bought up the Daimler patents and formed the Daimler Motor Co. in an enormous disused cotton mill in Coventry, but also proceeded to buy up the British rights of every existing patent. They bought up past, present, and future rights of the Count De Dion, they bought up the patents of Bolle, and having acquired all the best ideas of those two great French innovators who, outside the field of invention, had done more than anyone else to *develop* the motor-car, they then bought up everything else they could lay their hands on. They even succeeded in an action brought against the Hon. C. S. Rolls who paid them a royalty of £15 to use his Peugeot car which infringed their patent.

In 1895 Sir David Salomans organized a motor-car show on the Agricultural Showground at Tunbridge Wells in Kent. It was open for one day – October 15th – from 3 until 5 pm and was the first Motor Show in this country. In the following year H. J. Lawson organized a show at the Imperial Institute at South Kensington. The Prince of Wales and many others came to inspect the cars, but it was not in fact a motor-car at all which caused the sensation at that time but an electric brougham. This was the apotheosis of the horseless carriage, being in fact for all the world like a horsedrawn brougham but driven by electric motors. It must be remembered that at this time electricity was all the rage and the silence and efficiency of the electric engine was likely to be greatly in excess of its petrol equivalent. The facts that its range was pathetic and its speed non-existent were hardly causes for concern; and it was anyway intended for use almost entirely within the town.

Across the Channel, a very different story can be told. Production was developing in a very commercial manner and Panhard alone had an order book which was full for months ahead. Motor racing had started and in June 1895 the Paris–Bordeaux race of 732 miles was won by Levassor on a Panhard two cylinder at an average speed of 15 m.p.h. Indeed motor racing had become an everyday thing as anyone could have seen it would. Once the motor-car became available to the private owner, it was only a matter of time before one man was prepared to challenge another to show his prowess.

In fact it was at this time and in France that the motor-car as we know it really came into being. Emile Levassor was a partner of René Panhard and their firm was in business making band-saws. Daimler and Levassor had a mutual friend called Sarazin, a Belgian who had acquired the rights to sell Daimler engines in France. Sarazin talked Levassor into actually making engines and when he died his wife not only continued the business arrangement but married Levassor into the bargain – complete with a licence to build Daimler engines! But it was when Levassor came to design his own car that he in fact created the archetype of every car that has been made since. Up to that time it was fairly usual for a small one-or two-cylinder engine to be placed either in the rear of the car or under the seats. Drive was usually by belt or later by chain and the whole affair had a spindly look of a small horse-drawn buggy made of bicycle parts. By the time Levassor had finished with it it had the engine in the front under a bonnet, a clutch and a gear-box amidships, and a rear drive by differential to the back wheels; in other words, a motor-car with its mechanical parts disposed in a manner which we should nowadays call conventional.

It was at about this time that the great transatlantic dichotomy began. Unlike the Europeans, the Americans for many years continued to make the spindly single-cylinder motor-cars epitomized by what is known as the 'curved dash Olds', a car built by Oldsmobile which gave sterling service although possessed of only a 5 h.p. engine and minimal performance. However, it was not engineering which produced this dichotomy but the needs of the people. Whereas in Europe the motor-car remained a toy for the upper classes it rapidly became in America an essential part of their developing land. Although the railways had opened up the Middle West, farmers were still a long way from the nearest town and any means more reliable and quicker than a horse was to be welcomed.

Nevertheless, the way for the motor-car was not easy on either side of the Atlantic and in America the farmers' Anti-Automobile Society prepared the following measure for Congress suggesting that 'if a horse is unwilling to pass an automobile, the owner of the motorized vehicle should take the machine apart as rapidly as possible and conceal the parts in the bushes'.

It is pleasant to record that this measure was never seriously considered. On the other hand European peasantry and particularly the rural labourers in England suffered a great deal at the hands of the early automobilists and a Petition to Queen Victoria reads:

'May it please Your Majesty, the villagers of the United Kingdom beseech Your Majesty to help us get some relief from the motor-car. We are sure Your Majesty cannot know how much we suffer from them.

'They have made our lives a misery, our children are always in danger, our things are ruined in the dust, we cannot open our windows, our rest is spoiled by the noise at night. If they could be made to go slow through the villages it would be a great thing but we are only poor people and the great majority of those who use the car take no account of us. We do not know what to do and we appeal to Your Majesty to use Your great influence on our behalf.'

During the first decade of the twentieth century the development of the motor-car was astonishing in its rapidity. First, from the spindly two seats arose a generation of magnificent touring cars with open bodies and large all-weather hoods. The size of the bonnet increased and the height of the radiator rose and the power of the engine along with it. Chain drive disappeared, pneumatic tyres arrived. By 1905 closed coachwork was freely available if not exactly commonplace. By 1910 magnificent limousines designed for chauffeur driving were the order of the day and in 1911 the great six-cylinder 40 h.p. Renault first made its appearance – an immense and powerful vehicle. In 1906 the detachable rim arrived and punctures from then on became less of a menace. In 1907 Rolls-Royce produced the Silver Ghost, and Brooklands Motor Course, the great concrete saucer at Weybridge, Surrey, was first opened to the public. By 1908 interchangeable parts for assembly were a serious consideration and by 1909 the design of the radiator was developed to a point where it could be used to identify a make of car, a situation which was to last for something like forty years.

By 1910 the motor-car had established itself. The great transatlantic dichotomy was complete, for whereas there were owner drivers in Europe without question, the majority of cars were operated by a chauffeur. They were kept in the 'motor-house' and the fact that they were not actually fed on oats was carefully concealed from the drawing rooms of the gentry. On the other hand, in America, Henry Ford was pressing ahead with his mass production and some time before the outbreak of the Great War, the motor-car in America had already ceased to be an instrument of adventure and a mark of wealth, and had become as everyday as a cooking stove. By 1914 Ford were selling 248,307 cars a year at the fantastically low price of $490 each; and lady drivers were far from unknown.

Technically Europe was still undoubtedly in the lead; Ernest Henry had produced the twin overhead camshaft Peugeots, which although designed as racing cars were subsequently to influence the entire world of motoring. Vauxhall had produced the first of their Prince Henry Tourers and openly described it in advertisements as a sports car, thus creating an image which lives with us still. By 1913 or thereabouts the car was becoming more generally available in Europe and a number of small cars were produced, the running costs for which could be considered reasonable; the owner of a light car doing his own maintenance and vulcanizing his own punctures could hope to run a simple vehicle for something like £40 or £50 a year – the bulk of this cost being the cost of tyres.

The commercial vehicle, too, was under development and lorries were to be seen quite commonly on the roads, while London could boast of a fleet of motor-buses. By 1914 it could be seen that although only the rich as yet had the car, it was one day going to be available to all and sundry, and in America the development of mass production was already putting this thought into effect. By 1913 Morris was already offering his Oxford two seater fully equipped for £175 and in America Ford had introduced full-scale assembly-line production and made a quarter of a million cars in 1914. Even as the storm clouds gathered and the assassination at Sarajevo let slip the dogs of war, we must note that it was in a car that the killing took place. Whatever may be the debits of that great holocaust we cannot escape the fact that on the credit side it proved to be the greatest forcing ground for automobile development that could possibly have happened and the cars which came into being in the period after the war were fundamentally those which we drive about today. This was not only because the existing cars, taxis and buses were all forced into service in 1914; but more because the development of specialist vehicles such as the tank, and the full-scale four-wheel drive military lorries demanded by the mud, did much to improve suspension; while perhaps the internal combustion engine developed more particularly by its application to the aeroplane and the need for powerful and reliable aero engines in which Bugatti, Birkigt (Hispano-Suiza) and Bentley were all involved.

'We have the honour to be, Sir . . .'

The fascination of the advertisements in this first section which is to take us up to the outbreak of World War I, is that they exactly anticipate all that is to come in later years. Every idea and every cliché to which an unsuspecting public would eventually be expected to submit is here for inspection. This is a copywriter's bonanza with the poor designer as yet struggling to be born.

The advertisements' charm is only the charm of antiquity; there is little to delight the eye, though the Argyll catalogue for 1905 might perhaps be regarded as a trendsetter. The French posters have to be regarded in a light of their own, since they come in a period when the French poster has already become a collector's piece, and these are no less worthy than some of their counterparts devoted to the theatre, though Toulouse-Lautrec is not among their creators. Towards the very end of the section, when it might be said that the French had got into their style, there are some notable examples of good taste.

The difference of approach between the United States and Europe is evident even from the first two examples. The Duryea brothers were happy simply to announce that the motor vehicle was here and was available if you had the money to buy it; but the Great Horseless Carriage Co. addressed itself from the word 'go' – and 1896 can reasonably be regarded as the word 'go' – to the nobility and gentry. To them it 'had the honour to present'; and in retrospect one can see the first car salesman complete in his morning suit frantically washing his soapless hands in the shadows of Great Portland Street. Outside Great Britain the attitude was a little less obsequious, and from the earliest days the great Italian Fiat Company presented its motor-cars to the public with a sense of style and common sense which it was never to lose.

The Americans from the early days onwards remained immensely practical, and it was not until the sophistication of the 1930's that they were finally to give up their copy-laden advertisements designed to inform as much as to sell. By the turn of the century both safety and reliability were everyday selling points; and although the celebrated curved-dash Oldsmobile had become an anachronism it was still easily sold on the grounds of reliability alone – although the hilarious advertisement which claimed that Nature made a mistake giving the horse brains at least had the good grace to wonder if the owner would have any either! A sense of luxury had arrived in America within ten years of the introduction of the motor-car, but even so the Cadillac was not pressing its grandeur so much as its capabilities.

Fact and fiction. Only eight years separate the manufacturer's bald announcement on the opposite page from that of one of the early London dealers, above. The former 1888; the latter 1896.

On this side of the Atlantic a consciousness of the kind of person who was likely to buy the motor-car was in evidence not only in the restrained cover of the Argyll catalogue, but also in the kind of garden party invitation approach with which the management of C. S. Rolls & Co. offered their services to the public.

By 1906 the benefit of competitions was already a happy hunting ground in the agencies, and the Stanley Steam Car Co. had no hesitation in announcing that it had made the fastest car in the world. Two years later Mercedes were making the most of their success in the French Grand Prix and while the style of the advertisement belongs clearly to its period, the same advertisement has in fact been appearing consistently ever since.

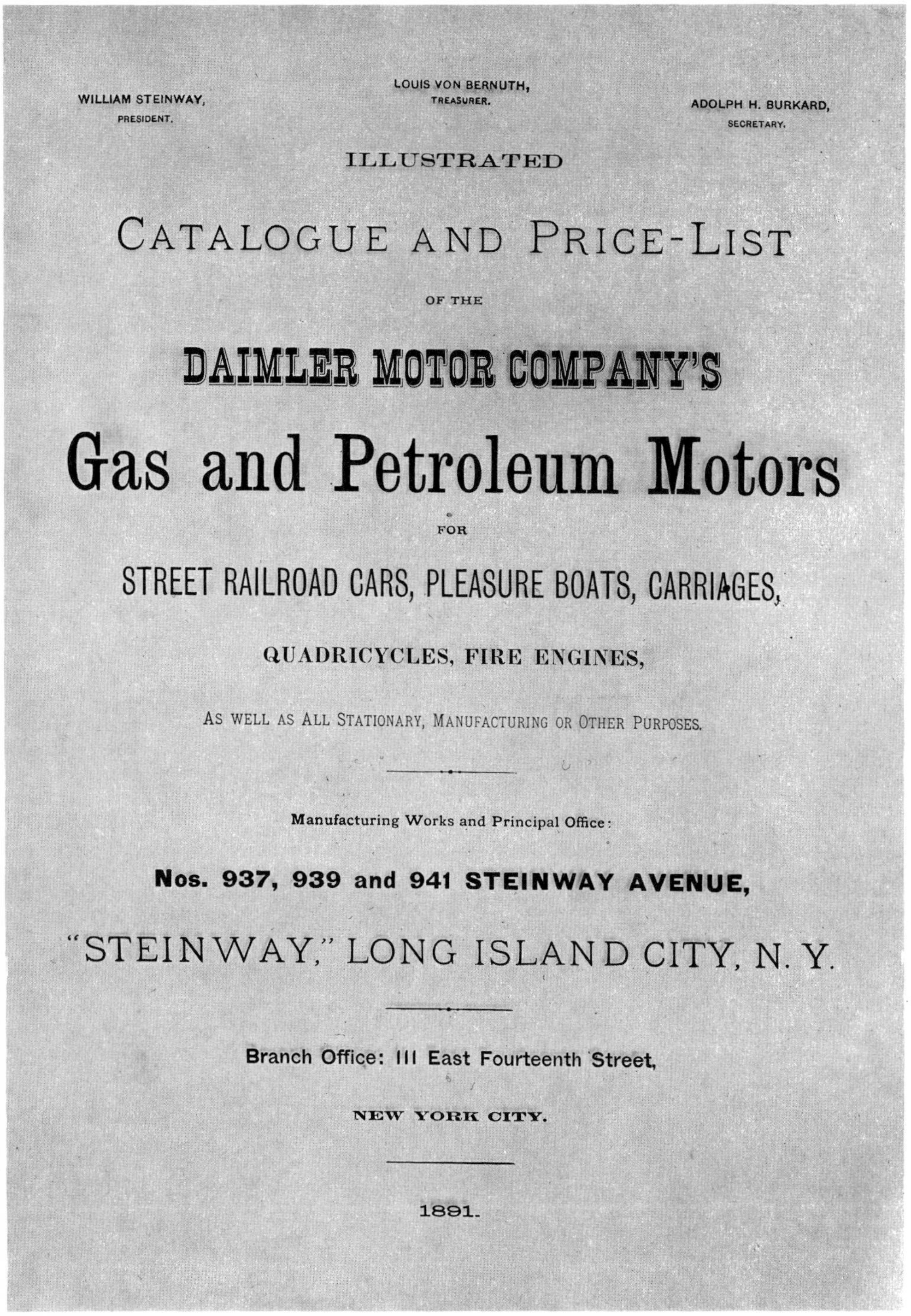

WILLIAM STEINWAY,
PRESIDENT.

LOUIS VON BERNUTH,
TREASURER.

ADOLPH H. BURKARD,
SECRETARY.

ILLUSTRATED

CATALOGUE AND PRICE-LIST

OF THE

DAIMLER MOTOR COMPANY'S

Gas and Petroleum Motors

FOR

STREET RAILROAD CARS, PLEASURE BOATS, CARRIAGES,

QUADRICYCLES, FIRE ENGINES,

AS WELL AS ALL STATIONARY, MANUFACTURING OR OTHER PURPOSES.

Manufacturing Works and Principal Office:

Nos. 937, 939 and 941 STEINWAY AVENUE,

"STEINWAY," LONG ISLAND CITY, N. Y.

Branch Office: 111 East Fourteenth Street,

NEW YORK CITY.

1891.

Stranger than fiction is the truth that the first serious effort to import motors into the United States was by the Steinway Piano Company – who of course already had German associations.

About this time we can sense the copywriters sitting scratching their heads for some new attribute which could be given to the car to boost the sales, and it was not long before silence became something worth talking about. It was of course silence for the user, and not the boon that Queen Victoria's villagers sought, which designers and copywriters were anxious to promote. That this particular attribute has now disappeared from the advertisement pages of the motor magazines is simply an acknowledgment of the fact that

America's first car – built and sold for a brief period by the Duryea Brothers – around 1892.

THE HORSELESS AGE.

DURYEA

MOTOR WAGON

* * COMPANY,

SPRINGFIELD, MASS.

MANUFACTURERS OF

Motor Wagons,

Motors, and * * *

Automobile Vehicles

of all kinds.

technical progress being what it is more or less any car nowadays is silent. All the same it is worth remembering that but a few years ago there was a deep and long drawn-out argument as to whether the new big Ford in America was in fact quieter than the Rolls-Royce; and whether in either case to hear the clock ticking was of any particular advantage. Towards the end of the decade, the lady driver began to come into her own, more so in America than in England, for in England the chauffeur was pretty much the mainstay of the

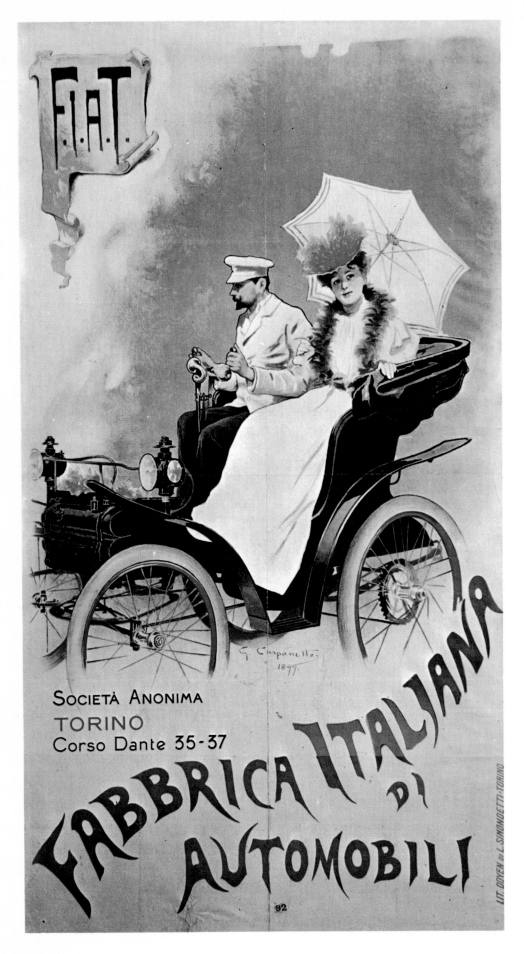

In the beginning (1899) even Fiat, who have almost always played down the social significance of car ownership, had to provide a chauffeur – or was he an archduke? The motoring dress of the day makes identification hazardous.

Opposite: No French poster artist of the grand period was going to allow a mere motor-car to change his sense of style – what was good enough for the Moulin Rouge would be good enough for the Société de Construction de L'Ouest!

The FORD

Our claim for the superiority of the FORD double opposed motor over the single cylinder is substantiated by the fact that without an exception all the $2,000 to $5,000 cars have two or more cylinders. The Ford gives greater satisfaction and equals in speed, reliability and comfort any car sold at less than $2,000.

PRICE WITH TONNEAU, $900.

We agree to assume all responsibility in any action the trust may take regarding the alleged infringement of the Selden Patent to prevent you from buying the Ford—"The Car of Satisfaction."

Write for Illustrated Catalogue and name of our nearest agent.

FORD MOTOR CO., Detroit, Mich.

Northern Automobiles

EIGHT HUNDRED DOLLARS

FOR speed, safety, and solid strength the **Northern** surpasses all other gasoline runabouts. The crowning triumph of twelve years of automobile building by a master mechanic. Perfectly constructed of the best materials, of beautiful design, superbly finished; odorless and noiseless; easy to start and operator has absolute control. There is every provision for comfort; big luxurious cushions; pivotal body bearings that insure a motion independent of the motor and combine with the springs to absorb all vibration. The sturdy **Northern Automobile** is a substantial product of a substantial company and has records for speed and endurance. Write for Catalog and name of nearest agent.

NORTHERN MANUFACTURING COMPANY, - - - **Detroit, Mich.**

The best and worst of American taste at the turn of the century. From the 'pun' on the left to the cartoon joke on the right one thing is clear – the car had arrived and it had arrived for everybody. The Oldsmobile seen outside the bank and exercising the dogs was one of the earliest successes of the American automobile industry and remained in production long after it was really obsolete simply because it was reliable.

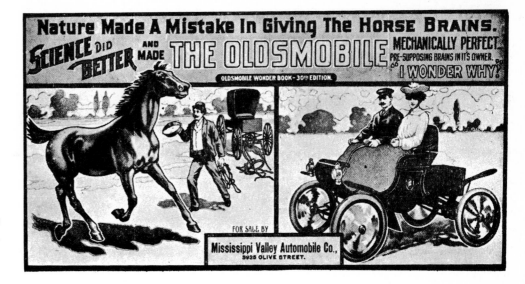

Nature Made A Mistake In Giving The Horse Brains. SCIENCE DID BETTER AND MADE THE OLDSMOBILE MECHANICALLY PERFECT. PRE-SUPPOSING BRAINS IN ITS OWNER. "I WONDER WHY?"

OLDSMOBILE WONDER BOOK - 30th EDITION.

FOR SALE BY

Mississippi Valley Automobile Co., 3935 OLIVE STREET.

Enter the Ladies – but despite all the advertisements seem to claim there were not many lady drivers, mostly because they found the cars so hard to start. The social implications on the opposite page do not bear thinking about; but the poor servant might have looked happier if the lady had paid more attention to her sense of direction and less to her headgear.

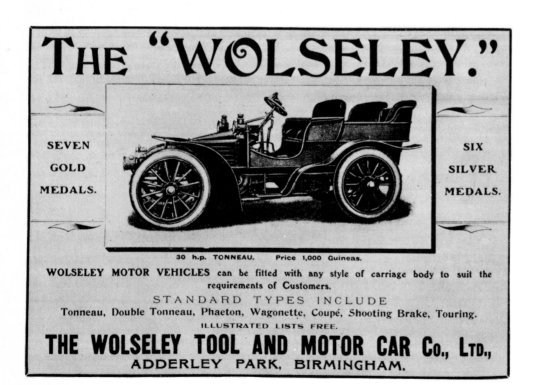

There is no
Prohibitive Grade
for the **CADILLAC**

The Cadillac Automobile will go up any grade of any well=traveled road, without balk—most=time without change of gear. The Cadillac does more than overcome grades—it is a machine for all roads and all seasons. Mr. I. L. Atwood, an auto novice, drove a Cadillac containing three passengers from New York to Waterbury, Conn., 93 miles, at an aver= age speed of 13 miles an hour without a stop. This is a typical

CADILLAC

performance— no accident, no repairs —but perfect satisfaction. No gaskets to burn or blow out; new sparking device endorsed by all gas-engine experts; same copper water jacket as used in latest French machines; speed range 4 to 30 miles an hour; only two places to oil— against 10 or more in others; interchangeable bronze bearings; mechanic- ally operated valves. Model A, 1904, with the Détachable Tonneau seating four *facing forward*, $850. Without tonneau, the smartest of Runabouts, $750. Our free illustrated booklet G gives address of agency nearest you where the Cadillac may be seen and tried.

CADILLAC AUTOMOBILE CO., Detroit, Mich.
Member Association of Licensed Automobile Manufacturers.

Style and performance. Here is one of the first 'performance' advertisements showing that by 1905 a car had to be better than its competitors if it was to sell. On the opposite page one of the first catalogues to show some sense of style.

motoring scene. However, as prices dropped and petrol became more readily available, the middle classes were soon to be found at the wheel.

By 1910 a quite considerable degree of sophistication had set in on both sides of the Atlantic. The cars themselves had moved on from their spindly beginnings into something at least resembling the motor vehicle as we understand it. Owner drivers had become reasonably common in Europe and common indeed in America. There was a wide range of products available in

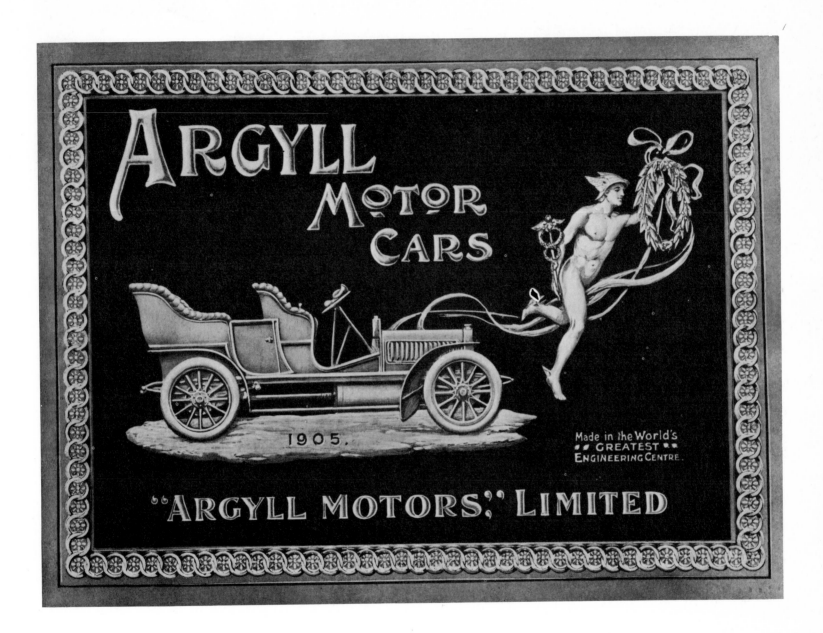

all parts of the world and a range of prices to go with them. On the one hand mere utility could no longer be regarded as enough, and on the other the frankly obsequious approach to the upper classes suggesting merely that the possession of a motor-car was a *sine qua non* would not do. On both sides of the Atlantic therefore we find a development in which the special delights of any particular model were what the advertisements sought to extol. In America the example given here of the Flanders Coupé from 1910 is typical

Ever widening claims. After performance comes amenity, for by 1907 the 'fun' had gone out of motoring – it had become a means of transport and ought as such to be acceptably comfortable.

A Practically Noiseless Car

SOME motor cars in motion sound like a boiler shop on a busy day. They creak, pound and groan with rheumatic regularity. Their running parts seem to be aching joints relieved only by these noisy evidences of mechanical ills and disordered make-ups.

Stoddard=Dayton

machines kick up no such fussy racket. They move along as smoothly as the grease and oil in which all running parts are packed. Every pound of power that is coming to you in speed and mileage is a certain Stoddard-Dayton WEARING ASSET.

In our Model-F 5-passenger touring car the noiseless qualities of preceding models have all been retained, and in our new Stoddard-Dayton 4-cylinder motor— cylinders cast in pairs—a perfect system of lubrication is maintained independent of splash.

The Stoddard-Dayton will equal the performance of any American-made car, at any price, as to speed, power, control and durability.

Model-F is a 30-35 H. P. high class car; transmission sliding gear, selective type, 3 speeds and reverse; 34 inch wheels; enclosed fenders; equipped with strut rods, which take all strain off rear springs, now hung on shackles at both ends.

Thoro tests prove higher efficiency of new motor 4⅝ x 5.
Price $2,500, including front and rear lamps. Our 1907 Auto-Book gives splendid description of all our machines. Let us send it to you—FREE.

THE DAYTON MOTOR CAR CO., DAYTON, OHIO.

of this development; having simply stated that it is silent and has an amply efficient engine, the rest of the copy is devoted to its comfort and the fact that it is 'a veritable drawing room on wheels'; it even carries some information as to colour. The question of colour is an interesting sideline. Henry Ford, practical to the end, must have made himself the arch-enemy of paint manufacturers by stating that you could have his car in any colour you liked as long as it was black. But even leaving this old joke to die its natural

1906: One of the first record claims – the first invitation to prospective owners to bask in the reflected glory.

S T A N L E Y   S T E A M   C A R

THE FASTEST CAR IN THE WORLD

(Rate of 127.66 Miles an Hour)

This car, at Ormond, Fla., Jan. 21 to 28, 1906, established the following World's Records:

WORLD'S RECORDS		FORMER RECORDS	
1 Kilometre	.18$\frac{2}{5}$	Darracq	.21$\frac{2}{5}$
1 Mile	.28$\frac{1}{5}$	Napier	.34$\frac{2}{5}$
1 Mile in Competition	.31$\frac{1}{5}$		.41$\frac{2}{5}$
5 Miles	2.47$\frac{1}{5}$	Napier	3.17
2 Miles (World's record for cars eligible under the rules)	.59$\frac{3}{5}$		

The 5-mile record was made in competition, with a scoring start, and was at the rate of a mile in 33$\frac{2}{5}$ seconds, which is faster than any gasolene car built according to A. A. A. rules ever made for a single mile.

The power-plant in this car is exactly like that in the regular Stanley cars, except that it is larger, of about twice the power as the Touring Cars (Model F). It weighs 1,600 pounds, and has margin enough for another boiler of the same size (512 pounds) without passing the racing weight-limit of 2,204 pounds. The boiler is 30 inches in diameter and 18 inches deep. It contains 1,475 tubes, and has a total heating surface of 285 square feet. A steam pressure of 800 to 900 pounds is carried. The engine is 4$\frac{1}{2}$ x 6$\frac{1}{2}$, and makes 350 revolutions to the mile. The wheels are 34 inches in diameter, and make 600 revolutions to the mile. They are equipped with 3-inch G. and J. tires. The body is so designed that the largest cross-section it presents, including the wheels, is only 9 square feet.

death, colour was something that does not really appear in motor-cars until well on into the 1920's. Cars took their lead presumably from the carriages that preceded them; and although one or two eccentrics managed bright yellow, or on occasion black and green stripes placed vertically (for motor-cars in those days were more vertical than horizontal), most of the paintwork, if not black, was very sober, and little account was taken of it. Later we shall have an opportunity in the section of this book which deals with the period

Not yet 'The best car in the world' but showing every sign that it was going to be (1910).

PERSONAL.

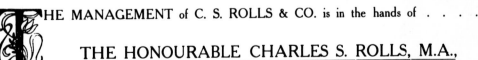

THE MANAGEMENT of C. S. ROLLS & CO. is in the hands of . . . .

THE HONOURABLE CHARLES S. ROLLS, M.A.,

and

MR. CLAUDE JOHNSON.

The Hon. C. S. Rolls & Mr. Claude Johnson, give personal attention to each order, and will, at all times, be pleased to personally interview clients as to their requirements, either at their offices in Conduit Street, or at clients' own residences.

Silent as an electric; amply efficient in its motive power; complete to the remotest detail in the refinement of its body; ready at any time to travel anywhere, the Flanders "20" Coupé is the ideal vehicle to carry Milady on her expeditions into the shopping district or on her round of social duties.

Its comfort makes it a veritable drawing room on wheels.

This Coupé is luxuriously equipped, is finished in dark green enamel with nickeled trimmings, has English broadcloth upholstering, and is fitted with interior and exterior electric lights.

The E-M-F Company
Automobile Manufacturers
Detroit, Mich.

FLANDERS 20 TWENTY

Coupé

$975

1910: The dawn of elegance – the beginning of background – and almost the first mention of colour, which had so far played little or no part in car salesmanship.

between the Wars, to examine some of the influences which came to bear upon motor-car advertising and indeed one suspects on the design of the motor-car itself.

Although these early days were days of extreme technical innovation, when every year produced a startling development, very little is made of this in any of the advertisements. On the face of it this is remarkable; on the one hand it can only be assumed that the number of purchasers was so small that they had

Within a few years of this 1911 advertisement the 'self-starter' had become an everyday fitment on even the cheaper cars; but here was the first answer to the maiden's prayer.

Any Woman Can Start your Car

"Crank From the Seat Not From the Street"

Did This Ever Strike YOU?

THE CRANK—
A Last Relic of Crudity and First Invention on the Otherwise Highly Perfected Modern Automobile and Motor Boat.

THE CRANK—
An Automobile Vermiform Appendix, Useless and Dangerous to Life and Limb—A Waster of Gasoline and the Cause of Unnecessary Wear and Tear on the Engine—because the fellow who gets his engine going by means of this primitive device is usually glad enough to let it go at that.

THE CRANK—
That Causes Discomfort and Profanity when the Engine Fails in Sleet, Snow, Rain and Mud. You know the old-fashioned crank!

The Star Safety Crank

positively removes every possibility of injury while cranking the car.
If your auto is equipped with a **Star Safety Crank** you need have no fear of breaking your arm or wrist, or hurting yourself in any of the many ways so familiar to all auto drivers, in case the engine "backfires."
The Star Safety Crank insures you against every kind of accident that might arise while using the ordinary old-fashioned crank.
Send today for our illustrated literature on this indispensable device.

Send today for our illustrated booklet describing the Star Starter—a device which cranks your engine from the seat and one which is now largely doing away with the old-fashioned and dangerous methods of cranking.

We offer in the Star Starter a safe and thoroughly dependable method of cranking the car.

It is not necessary to leave the seat, and you can start and stop your engine at will, thus avoiding much loss in the items of gasoline—of engine wear and tear.

The whole thing is so beautifully simple and so convenient that no car owner should hesitate to investigate it and find out for himself exactly what it will do.

The Star Starter eliminates all danger of broken arms, sprains and injuries which frequently arise from the premature starting of the car—and we need not tell automobilists that these accidents are very frequent and serious.

The next time you start to crank your engine in the old-fashioned way just stop and consider how much trouble you could save yourself, how much freedom from danger of accident you could enjoy if your car was equipped with this equal and necessary engine starter.

Do not delay, but send for the booklet to-day. You can then possess yourself of full information, not only concerning the Star Starter, but also concerning the Star Safety Crank, another useful and very convenient device manufactured by us.

We want every car owner who is interested in an easy, effective and absolutely sure way of starting his engine, to get this illustrated literature on the subject.

The Star Starter Company

General Offices: 170 Broadway, New York City   Factory: Rochester, N. Y.

each and every one of them some idea of how the motor-car was developing and, on going to buy a new one, would accept that it was necessarily better than the previous model. This presumably was not anything to feature in an advertisement. Alternatively one can take the view that most of the motorists knew so little about the motor-car, its design or its construction, that there was little point in trying to appeal to their knowledge in this respect. At all events the great bug-bear of motoring in the early days was the incidence of

1913 BERLIET DETACHABLE WIRE WHEELS — PATENT

MR. BERLIET, realising the demand for these, is now — after prolonged tests — manufacturing a most perfectly designed detachable wheel. These can be fitted to all our chassis.

They are constructed throughout in our Works at Lyons, where we have laid down a special plant for the purpose, and the material used in their manufacture has been selected after exhaustive tests in our own Laboratory.

The general principle is similar to that adopted by other manufacturers of detachable wheels, the four inner hubs being permanently fixed to the

Sophistication both in mechanics and in appearance came well before the Great War. Here, in 1913, an acceptance of the fact that the men at least knew how a car worked and the ladies, God bless 'em, knew how to use it.

The influence of Royalty and racing. King Alfonso of Spain was even prepared to give his name to the sporting Hispano-Suiza, despite his ministers' view that this was undignified, while Mercedes brought their own ideas on dignity to capitalize on their first Grand Prix win – a process they have kept up ever since.

punctures, and the pneumatic tyre in its earliest form was a far from reliable thing, most motoring expeditions being bedevilled by the necessity to stop and change the tyre or, indeed, to be more accurate, to repair it and replace it. The one technical innovation, therefore, which seems to have made its mark in the advertisements was that of the detachable wheel or in America the detachable rim.

However, from the point of view of design there is quite a considerable development to be perceived by the turn of the first decade. One of the most interesting aspects of this is concerned with background. Whereas in the earliest advertisements it was sufficient merely to show the general shape of the car, from about 1910 onwards we see it in a setting; and the social implications of possessing it begin to matter. The Flanders advertisement places the car in an elegant portion of the city, and very soon after that we begin to see it before the imposing gates of a country house. This cult which began presumably in Europe was quickly followed in America and it can be traced in its varying stages throughout this book. Indeed the most remarkable thing perhaps is that no matter how much the shape of the motor-car changes, the shape of the establishment before which it is photographed or drawn remains almost exactly the same. In the earliest examples there seems little social implication; it is simply a background which appears in general terms to be suitable, appropriate, and, in the case of many of the chauffeur-driven limousines, even likely. However, in the next section of the book we shall see this develop into an astute sociological gambit. We shall be confronted by the eight-litre Bentley in front of the Casino at Monte Carlo, and more or less

MERCEDES

GRAND PRIX
1908 A.C.F. 1908

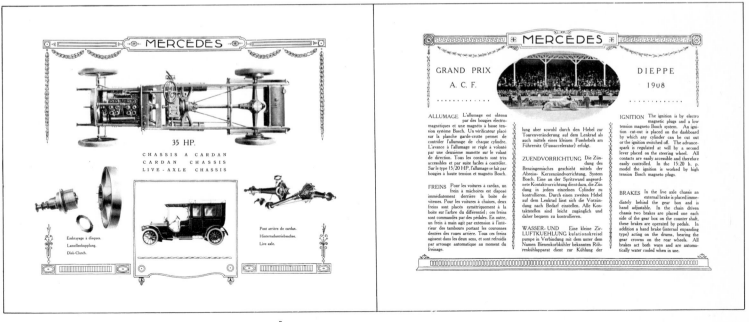

MERCEDES

35 HP.

CHASSIS A CARDAN
CARDAN CHASSIS
LIVE-AXLE CHASSIS

Embrayage à disques.
Lamellenkupplung.
Disk-Clutch.

Pont arrière de cardan.
Hinterradantriebsachse.
Live axle.

MERCEDES

GRAND PRIX
A. C. F.

DIEPPE
1908

ALLUMAGE L'allumage est obtenu par des bougies electro-magnetiques et une magnéto à basse tension système Bosch. Un vérificateur placé sur la planche garde-crotte permet de contrôler l'allumage de chaque cylindre. L'avance à l'allumage se règle à volonté par une deuxième manette sur le volant de direction. Tous les contacts sont très accessibles et par suite faciles à contrôler. Sur le type 15/20 HP, l'allumage se fait par bougies à haute tension et magnéto Bosch.

FREINS Pour les voitures à cardan, un frein à mâchoires est disposé immédiatement derrière la boite de vitesses. Pour les voitures à chaines, deux freins sont placés symétriquement à la boite sur l'arbre du différentiel; ces freins sont commandés par des pédales. En outre, un frein à main agit par extension à l'intérieur des tambours portant les couronnes dentées des roues arrière. Tous ces freins agissent dans les deux sens, et sont refroidis par arrosage automatique au moment du freinage.

lung aber sowohl durch den Hebel zur Tourenveränderung auf dem Lenkrad als auch mittels eines kleinen Fusshebels am Führersitz (Fussaccelerator) erfolgt.

ZUENDVORRICHTUNG Die Zündung des Benzingemisches geschieht mittels der Abreiss- Kerzenzündvorrichtung, System Bosch. Eine an der Spritzwand angeordnete Kontaktvorrichtung dient dazu, die Zündung in jedem einzelnen Cylinder zu kontrollieren. Durch einen zweiten Hebel auf dem Lenkrad lässt sich die Vorzündung nach Bedarf einstellen. Alle Kontaktstellen sind leicht zugänglich und daher bequem zu kontrollieren.

WASSER- UND LUFTKUEHLUNG Eine kleine Zirkulationskreisel pumpe in Verbindung mit dem unter dem Namen Bienenkorbkühler bekannten Röhrenkühlapparat dient zur Kühlung der

IGNITION The ignition is by electro magnetic plugs and a low tension magneto Bosch system. An ignition cut-out is placed on the dashboard by which any cylinder can be cut out or the ignition switched off. The advance-spark is regulated at will by a second lever placed on the steering wheel. All contacts are easily accessible and therefore easily controlled. In the 15/20 h. p. model the ignition is worked by high tension Bosch magneto plugs.

BRAKES In the live axle chassis an external brake is placed immediately behind the gear box and is hand adjustable. In the chain driven chassis two brakes are placed one each side of the gear box on the counter shaft, these brakes are operated by pedals. In addition a hand brake (internal expanding type) acting on the drums, bearing the gear crowns on the rear wheels. All brakes act both ways and are automatically water cooled when in use.

DOUBLE " BERLINE " ON 30 HP CHASSIS

30 HP CHASSIS
4 CYLINDERS 100 × 150

STANDARD SPECIFICATION

Motor : two " en bloc ", two cam shafts and interchangeable valves placed symetrically :: Plugs over centre of cylinders :: Petrol tank at rear maintained under constant pressure by special pump and patent pressure regulator (patent) :: Water circulation by centrifugal pump :: Gear box, four speeds and reverse, gate change :: Cooling, Ignition, Lubrication, Clutch, Transmission, Springs and Brakes as in all other types :: Artillery wheels.

CHASSIS   SPECIFICATION

Specification	Short	Long
Wheel base	9' 10"	10' 8"
Track	4' 7"	4' 7"
Length of frame available for body work	8' 2"	9' 0"
Length of frame from dash to centre of back wheels .	5' 7"	6' 5"
Width of chassis	2' 10"	2' 10"
Approximate weight of chassis	17 cwt.	18 cwt.
Speed per hour with torpedo body	70	66 ⅓
Price of chassis without tyres	£ 540	£ 570
Wheels for tyres of	880 by 120	880 by 120

(For Extras see page 21)

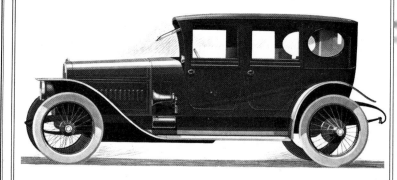

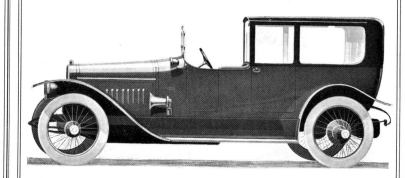

'We have the honour to be, Sir . . .'

The inter-relation of snobbery. Luxury on the left matched by an 'artist's impression' of the photograph on page 64.

any American car in a setting usually well beyond the means of its probable purchaser.

Lastly, in terms of their design, the advertisements, or more particularly the catalogues, improve as the car itself becomes a more interesting shape. As the vertical emphasis of the first motor-cars gives way to the long horizontal line, we eventually arrive at some really extravagant essays in which the designers of the catalogue themselves seem to have taken wing. In this period at the beginning of the life of the motor-car, one or two of the catalogues are worth looking at simply and solely for the element of draughtsmanship which appears in them. Here are line drawings worth looking at as line drawings. Here is printing worth looking at for its own sake, as a technique of reproduction. Here suddenly the designing tortoise overtakes the copywriting hare. It will not be until after the Great War that keeping up with the Joneses becomes part of life and what a change those wretched Joneses will make to the world of advertising, and indeed to the world of the motor-car.

The motor car comes of age: 1919-39

'Not all that tempts your wand'ring eyes
'And heedless hearts, is lawful prize;
'Nor all that glisters, gold.'
THOMAS GRAY
Ode on the Death of a Favourite Cat

However marvellous we now think our motor-cars, or come to that our advertising, there are strong arguments to suggest that the period between the two world wars was in fact the finest hour for both. For the motor-car emerged from the Great War more or less complete as we know it today, and was developed over the period of the next twenty-five years in such a way that practically every technical innovation we now enjoy was introduced during that period; what is more, a great deal of the splendour which that period also gave us has subsequently disappeared. In terms of advertising it is doubtful if much more has been achieved. Certainly the designers of today do not enjoy the reputation of those few who were the leaders of style and fashion in the period between the wars.

In 1918, all over Europe and in America, demobilized servicemen were returning home to enjoy the lands fit for heroes to live in. And the hero's life was not really thought to be complete without a motor-car. Indeed service life had brought the advantages of motoring to the attention of all and sundry – many had learnt how to control the beasts and an almost equal number how to service and maintain them. The world was full of factories which, though designed to produce the weapons of war, must now produce an alternative; and since ploughshares were not greatly in demand the motor-car was a fairly obvious alternative. All over Europe and America small mushroom firms sprang up, making motor-cars of widely different types and varieties, many of them appallingly bad, quite a few astonishingly good; and although the great masters, Ford and General Motors in America and to some extent Morris and Austin in Great Britain, were taking advantage of the new-found techniques of mass production, greatly developed during the previous four years, the motor-car could still reasonably be assembled by hand and no great expenditure was required on jigs and tools for pressed steel bodies – this was a nightmare yet to come. This technique of hand assembly, which should not be confused with what we usually refer to as a handbuilt car, was at root the reason for the wide diversity of motor-cars in the immediate post-war period. Before the advent of mass production and the use of the assembly line, it was customary to build cars by having a number of men (usually four or six) work round a chassis. This was first of all placed on four wooden blocks. The men would then go to the store and draw four wheels and fit them on. They would get an engine and test it and put it in. Many of the components came complete from outside the factory but the thing was put together by the same four men who did the whole job instead of one man, as in the case of mass production, simply putting a nearside front wheel on every chassis as it passed him. It does not betoken a tremendous amount of care, although possibly there was less room for error than in the early mass-production techniques. However, it cannot be compared with the kind of 'Rolls-Royce' attitude that people usually mean when they talk of a handbuilt car – in the sense that the Americans would use the expression 'custom built'. However, from the point of view of the small firms concerned, the great advantage was that no enormous outlay was necessary on tools and equipment and anyone who could raise a small amount of capital and get a large enough building to house a number of men could go into the business of producing motor-cars. They ranged from the eccentric and exciting to the merely everyday, with between those two extremes the solid kind of motor-car that Vauxhall, Talbot, Sunbeam, and others were making in the United Kingdom, the rather uninspired French family saloons, and the plethora of box-like sedans with which the American market was quickly flooded.

Looking back it is obviously the best which come to mind. Before the end of the 1920's the Duesenberg was in production in America. The great Hispano-Suizas and the immense Mercedes were already dominating the European scene. Henry Royce had produced the Phantom II and the large Double Six Daimlers were already employed by the British Royal Family.

Against this there was a mass of mundane motors for Mr and Mrs Jones. The best of them were remarkable for their common sense and reliability. Herbert Austin had introduced the Austin 7, a jingling squat little thing that at least brought motoring within the reach of (nearly) all. Slightly above and beyond this Morris was doing well with both his Cowley and Oxford models and so were such rarities as the Clyno, which did not long survive. All these offered ordinary family motoring for the ordinary family man.

Sanity demands that from this point onwards the catalogue of names should cease. The many, many volumes already written on the motor-cars of this period still leave the subject unexhausted. There are, however, practical short cuts which will enable us to see what occurred while avoiding the pitfalls of over enthusiasm and technical abstraction.

It is probably a useful beginning to look at the mechanical developments to see what actually happened during this period and how much of it has survived. We start with a conventional car. In the very early period after the war it was usually an open four seater with a canvas hood, powered by a four- or six-cylinder engine with side valves, driving through a conventional three- or four-speed gear-box to a back axle with differential. The wheels were frequently wire, but otherwise of artillery construction; that is to say, steel wheels with eight to twelve good thick spokes; a good example most easily recalled is the Morris Cowley. In America it was customary to use wooden spoked wheels with detachable rims. Both employed internal expanding brakes at first only on the rear wheels but subsequently on all four. Solid axles were employed both front and rear, and half-elliptical springs dampened by friction shock absorbers. It is to this basic model that the developments must now be added. To begin with, all the bodywork was assembled by hand, only such simple things as doors being previously pressed. Quite soon, however, the pressed steel body began to come into being. At first the techniques severely limited the shape; and the highly conventional box-like designs, which originated in America, and which can be found on Morris in England, on Renault and Citroën in France, Opel in Germany, and Fiat in Italy, were not so much the slavish copying of one design by another designer, but sprang from the limitations of the techniques as then understood.

As far as the engines were concerned, although the majority of them remained for many years with conventional side valves, or, as the Americans would say, L-head units, most of the subsequent developments were already in fact in being. Ever since Peugeot had put the twin overhead camshaft on his racing cars, a number of production cars had followed suit. The most notable was probably the twin-cam three-litre Sunbeam, available in the mid-twenties. There were, of course, a number of overhead valve designs, particularly the overhead camshaft Bentleys, and quite a wide variety of designs incorporating pushrods. Bentley used a strange eccentric design which was a strong reminder that he served his apprenticeship at Doncaster in the railway workshops; this kind of mechanical device is not uncommon in steam engines. In the late 1920's Georges Roesch introduced on his Talbot cars engines with pushrod operated valves using a unique rocker mechanism which enabled him to save a good deal of weight. He can be credited with developing the fast 'revving' engine for everyday use and for raising the compression ratios much nearer the standard employed today. Against this fairly conventional development can be placed the eccentric marvels of Ettore Bugatti who all along ploughed his own furrow, and was a long time coming to twin overhead camshafts. Also against the run of the mill were the vast Mercedes cars with superchargers blowing through the carburettor. But all these are eccentricities. The straightforward line of development was from side to pushrod operated overhead valves, thus raising compression ratios and making use of higher revolutions, until we find at the end of the period just before the outbreak of the Second World War engines which lead logically to those we use today.

In suspension the development was slower, but by the mid-thirties Buick had introduced what they were pleased to call 'knee-action'. This in fact was independent front suspension; and in the last five years before the Second World War it became very general indeed. (At this point it must be clearly stated that this was not really a new development – independent suspension had been in use almost as long as the motor-car but not in *general* use.) Looked at in the light of today's knowledge most of the systems introduced during the late 1930's were appalling in their design. Few of them kept the front wheels in anything like a straight line and the variation in angle between the tyre and the road produced more wear than most of us would nowadays like to contemplate. Furthermore the systems did little to improve the road holding of the cars. The most that can be said of them was that they added considerably to the comfort of the passengers, provided, and only provided, that the car was driven in a moderate manner. A few European manufacturers were beginning to develop independent rear suspension, but this was usually of swing axle design which resulted in hair-raising handling qualities in all but the most straightforward circumstances. Once more a few eccentrics such as Bugatti went their own way, Bugatti himself remaining faithful to 'cart springs' but damped by some of the most expensive shock absorbers ever made.

The greatest strides probably came in the sphere of transmission, a part of the car with which the owner was much concerned. For the technique of changing gears on a crash gear-box with a conventional clutch was not easily acquired; and even the most practised motorist was wont to accept that every now and then he would make a nasty crunch as he moved from one gear to another. In the very late 1920's Armstrong Siddeley introduced the self-changing gear-box, a device for which its later description of pre-selector is much more accurate. A quadrant under the steering wheel enabled the gear to be selected, but the actual change did not take place until what was substituted for the clutch pedal was depressed. This device was much improved by Daimler who added a fluid flywheel having some of the qualities of a torque converter and also acting as clutch. Also at this time the free wheel became available which at least made it unnecessary to depress the clutch during gear changes when the car was on the move; but in fact at the same time it removed all traces of engine braking and therefore placed a considerable strain on the brakes which were not then what they are today. Synchro-mesh became general from the thirties onwards, so that the real difficulties of gear changing had probably disappeared anyway. Also in the early thirties came a few eccentricities such as the Hayes Automatic transmission, of which only one example has survived. This was a completely automatic arrangement of great complexity and little reliability. Towards the end of the thirties, another device of electro-magnetic design appeared from France known as the Cotal gear-box.

In the light of these developments the Americans appeared to be rather slow off the mark, contenting themselves with ordinary synchro-mesh, although a number of vehicles introduced an electrically operated gear-box in which the actual gear lever was replaced by a small miniature affair situated on a cross arm below the steering wheel. But this was in fact a difference in operation rather than a difference in design. Just before the outbreak of the Second World War, the Americans began to introduce the automatic gear-box as we know it today, a combination of epicyclic trains coupled to a hydraulic torque converter. Somewhere in the middle of all this purely mechanical development came the monocoque body shell which dispensed with the conventional chassis altogether, in Europe anyway, and it is a careful blending of all these kinds of development which provided another step towards giving us the motor-car as we know it now.

Suffice it to say for the purposes of this book that by 1939 it had all happened. More interesting perhaps to many than these mere technical facts is the kind of effect they had on the motor-car and the people who used it. Here for the sake of simplicity we can assume three general classes: the great and luxurious was still only for the very rich; the middle range was bought by what we should now call professional and executive men, and the small everyman's car, although still limited to people with some kind of financial freedom, was already bringing motoring to the lower ends of the social scale. One curious point remains. In Europe these cars were easily definable by size as much as anything else, but, although the same three categories in fact existed in America, the size of the vehicles remained more or less the same, as indeed in many respects did their appearance. To an unpractised eye there is very little difference between a 1932 Cadillac and a 1932 Chevrolet, except the price ticket where the difference was very marked; but the most simple-minded man can readily tell the difference between a 1932 Rolls-Royce and a 1932 Austin 7.

On both sides of the Atlantic the big and expensive models tended to fall into two categories. There were the limousines, the chauffeur-driven cars of extremely conventional appearance, large in size in order to make them comfortable, powerful in order to make them quiet rather than fast, luxurious in their trim and appurtenances in the rear half and spartan in the front one. Against this there were a number of exotic cars for what we should nowadays presumably call the 'jet-set'. These cars, especially in the latter half of the period, represent an era which seems totally to have passed. They were almost invariably, even in America, equipped with specially built bodies frequently to the design of their prospective owners or, should we say more accurately, to a design approved by their prospective owners. As often as not they were two seaters, even though the chassis had originally been planned to hold a limousine of immense proportions, and had only occasionally been shortened to meet its other requirement. One two-seater was even built on the Bugatti Royale chassis which itself had a wheelbase of rather more than 15 ft, and a track of about 5 ft 6in. This was in fact built to the order of a Mr Armand Esders, and was not equipped with lights of any kind since this gentleman did not believe in motoring in the dark! It was in fact the French who at this period made the most of this demand for special and particularly beautiful cars, and some half-dozen or more coachbuilding firms sprang up near Paris devoted entirely to producing the most flamboyant and remarkable vehicles. Towards the end of the thirties the effect of their work was beginning to show not only in France, but in other places as well, in the design of cars for the upper middle range, but with the coming of the Second World War this type of vehicle disappeared more or less completely. It disappeared because the way of life of which it formed part also disappeared. One can hardly resist the temptation to sum the whole situation up in a paragraph from a letter written by M. Paul on behalf of Ettore Bugatti to Prince Mohammed Abdel Said in which he said: 'For such a special chassis I have never considered it necessary to publish a catalogue. There is in fact no need whatever of advertising such a model the prospective buyers of which, who are essentially aristocratic, are inaccessible by the means adopted for standard cars.'

By contrast, the middle range of cars continued to appear unobtrusive and conventional. They offered quality rather than flamboyance, modest performance, and reasonable economy. They are perhaps epitomized by say Humber in Great Britain and Buick in the United States. They were not cheap but they were good and there was little about their design which paid even lip service to improving the social standing of their owner, although, as we shall see, the advertisements were beginning to be conscious of the motor-car as a status symbol; and in the fullness of time the design department, urged on no doubt by the sales department, would be forced to consider what advertising men were already saying.

The little cars started immediately after the Great War as cycle cars, a terrible combination, half motor-car, half motor-cycle, with all the evils of both brought fully to the fore. Developing techniques, however, and the strong influence of Herbert Austin's famous Seven soon made them more conventional and more acceptable. Morris and Ford in England particularly did much to develop this type of car, and in Italy the Fiat Company introduced in the late 1930's the little 500 c.c. model which came to be known as the Topolino, or Mickey Mouse, and which really took the first step towards making the mini car as we know it today. Anticipating the ubiquitous 'Mini' they found favour as a second car for the rich as well as basic transport for the poor. And for many the discovery of the delights of such a small vehicle made them very attractive as 'fun' cars.

Unexciting as these little beasts may have been, they were ultimately reliable, economical, and within reasonable limits comfortable. At least they could take four people or two parents and two children from home to the seaside, and many more adventurous souls were quite prepared to use them for far longer journeys. They brought one new side issue with them. Some of them were soon developed into miniature sports cars and although the real enthusiast of the day might have looked down from the lofty grandeur of his four-and-a-half-litre Bentley and referred to them as 'buzz boxes' the original M.G. Midget and the Singer Nine Le Mans, to name only two, were cars which were profoundly to affect the development of the motor-car in later years. So much for the cars; what price their image when the ad men had finished with them.

'Ask the man who owns one.'

In terms of design and indeed in terms of copywriting this is the period of flamboyance, and although a serious look at the advertisements which appear on the following pages shows quite clearly that there is no development which was not anticipated in the period before the war, the degree of sophistication and the excellence of the design put it in a class apart. This is of course the period of 'Bébé' Berard, of Marcel Vertes, and all their hangers on, a kind of *de luxe* and acceptable French 'chocolate box' school, and it is also the period which came under the influence of Picasso, of cubism, of plain 'modern' art, and of a number of very powerful and individualistic typographers. It is the era of the young Noel Coward, and of the Black Bottom. The era when the young Ashley Havinden could break away from realism to launch the new winged Chryslers in Europe, the era when McKnight Kauffer and Eric Frazer were household names in smart drawing rooms. The era when the designers of Diaghilev's ballets ruled the roost.

Not unnaturally, after some of the excitements of the early part of this period, there was a swing in the mid-thirties to typographical severity, when, at least for the top manufacturers, no one would deign to put a picture of a car anywhere in their advertisement – and how they copied one another. As soon as Rolls-Royce had managed with nothing but words all the world must follow suit, until within two years panic had seized them and splendid photographs reappeared, the airbrush providing a gloss that no manufacturer could ever hope to achieve. Scraper board drawings came and, mercifully, went.

In the period immediately after the war, the advertisements, like the motor-cars, closely resembled their pre-war precursors. They hovered between the technique of plain announcement and the rather lush photograph in front of the country house. There is evidence too that in this doldrum period the printers took a firm hand. There is a period of fancy borders and printers' decorations, particularly in the world of catalogues, which shows quite clearly that where generally speaking tradition was being thrown to the winds, in printing at least some sense of craftsmanship remained. And one also sees that for some years to come a sense of craftsmanship remained with most of the motor-car manufacturers. There is a feeling, however, which cannot be escaped, that the door of the design department was firmly locked against the onslaught of the sales manager. Not so, however, the door of the advertising department, for although the cars continued their modest way,

Maibohm

Whizzing Speed! peaceful idling—
it makes a fellow's blood tingle
to look at a car like this and
feel that it belongs to him—
unleashed it will roar nose to
nose with an express train:
checked it will glide along
composedly behind a mule
team: a spirited car, ravenous
to devour the miles: a gentle,
soothing car, mild as a kitten:
coachwork with the symmetry
of a Rembrandt: springs that
lull where others crash—upholstery from a cow's back—the
lightest good six made.

Maibohm, Sandusky, Ohio
Maker of Fine Vehicles for 21 Years

Post-war divergence. It is difficult to 'tingle'
over the Maibohm even if the owner did;
but both the car and the advertisement are
straightforward. Below it one of the early
Voisin efforts. Gabriel Voisin, who was as
much aviator as motorist, used the strange
winged bird on all his radiators until the
outbreak of the Second World War when
he ceased to manufacture cars under his own
name – the chick is a mystery. On the
opposite page another mystery is explained –
an American maker's effort in 1916 when
European manufacture had ceased.

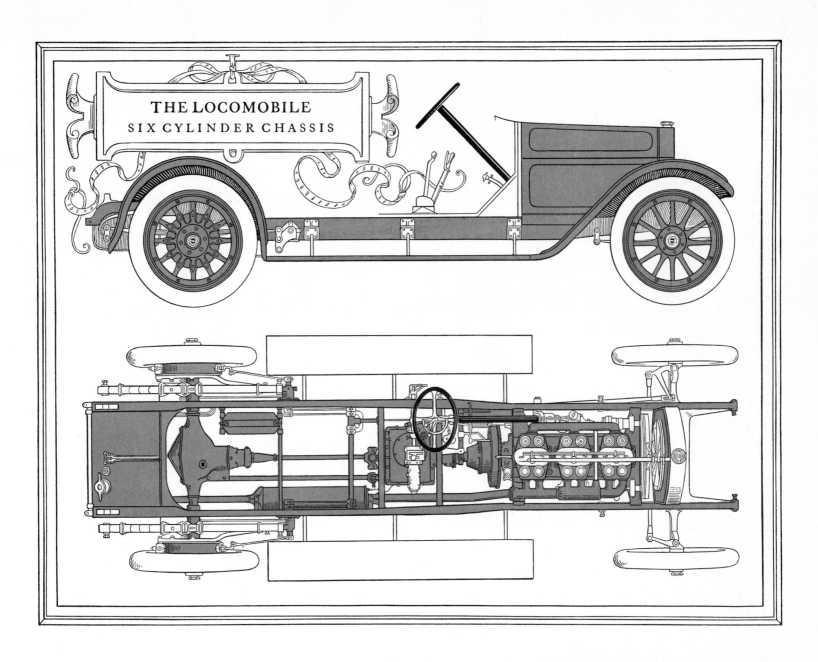

THE LOCOMOBILE
SIX CYLINDER CHASSIS

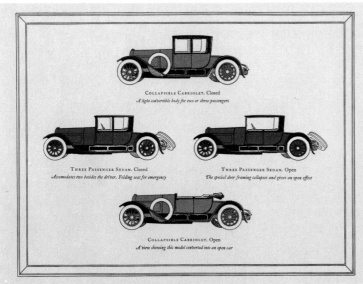

COLLAPSIBLE CABRIOLET. Closed
A light convertible body for two or three passengers

THREE PASSENGER SEDAN. Closed
Accommodates two beside the driver. Folding seat for emergency

THREE PASSENGER SEDAN. Open
The special door framing collapses and gives an open effect

COLLAPSIBLE CABRIOLET. Open
A view showing this model converted into an open car

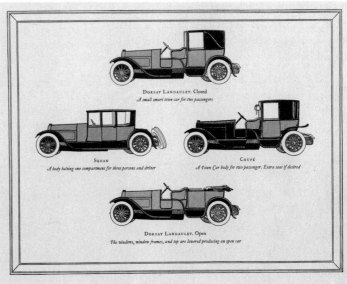

DORSAY LANDAULET. Closed
A small smart town car for two passengers

SEDAN
A body having one compartment for three persons and driver

COUPÉ
A Town Car body for two passenger. Extra seat if desired

DORSAY LANDAULET. Open
The windows, window frames, and top are lowered producing an open car

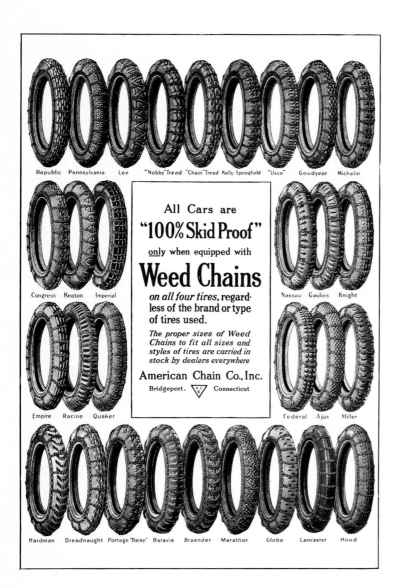

THE THREE LITRE
BENTLEY SPEED MODELS

 O car can put forward more convincing proofs of its speed and endurance than the Three Litre Speed Model Bentley, and its outstanding performances were attained with a model the design of which has never been radically altered. It was in June 1922 that three Bentley cars were taken from the production shops, and in their standard form were entered in the Tourist Trophy Race in the Isle of Man. They finished second, fourth, and fifth, and were the only team to complete the course, all the competitors being specially built racing models.

In September of the same year Capt. J. F. Duff on another standard Speed model covered 2,083 miles in two periods of 12 hours each, averaging 86.79 m.p.h. The Double Twelve-hour record was thus secured, and this performance remains unbeaten to-day, though many attempts have been made to improve on the figures.

In June 1924, at Le Mans, France, an ordinary Speed model with fully equipped four-seater body covered 1,380 miles in a continuous run of 24 hours, winning the Grand Prix d'Endurance. Throughout this gruelling test of day and night driving no mechanical trouble whatsoever was experienced.

The latest and finest achievement was the capturing of the World's 24-hours' Record at Montlhery, France, on 21st/22nd September, 1925. A production model privately owned by Capt. J. F. Duff and driven alternately by him and Capt. Woolf Barnato covered 2,280 miles at an average speed of 95.04 m.p.h. This chassis was the latest type speed model described herein.

It is only from tests such as these that the quality of a car can be proved, for in no case was a specially built model used.

A confusion of styles – and yet a curious
similarity. On the right the emergence of a
radiator shape as a 'trademark'.

The 'Touring' by Bentley (artist: Gordon Crosby) – one of the 'greats' of motoring. The 'Traditional' for Packard out of Madison Avenue and the 'Diplomatic' as an afterthought for the same manufacturer.

"The walls must get the weather stain before they grow the ivy" – And so with motor cars – The Packard Doorway, ivy-covered, typifies Packard's thirty years of experience in building fine motor cars and in making possible a Heritage of Good Design

"The walls must get the weather stain before they grow the ivy."
ELIZABETH BARRETT BROWNING

The Packard Standard Eight
The Sedan
Seven Passengers

Plate 6

A FEW VOISIN CUSTOMERS

M. Millerand, President of the French Republic.
Madame Millerand.
H. M. Alexandre Iᵉʳ, King of the Serbians, Croates and Slovaques.
H. M. the Queen of Romania.
M. de Alvear, President of the Argentine Republic.
H. M. Moulaï Youssef, Sultan of Morocco.
H. M. the Bey of Tunis.
H. R. H. the Prince Kitto, hereditary Prince of the Imperial Throne of Japan.
The hereditary Prince to the Throne of Romania.
H. R. H. the Prince of Siam.
H. R. H. the Prince Monheim of Egypt.
H. H. the Chambellan of the Sultan of Morocco.
H. R. H. Princess Helen of Greece.
M. Le Trocquer, Minister of Public Works.
M. Leon Bérard, Minister of Public Instruction.
M. Peyronnet, Minister of Public Works.
M. François Arago, Vice-President of the Chambre des Députés.
M Dan Brostrom, Minister of Marine in Sweden.
M. Dutasta, Former Ambassador, General Secretary of the Peace Conference.
M G Carlier, Minister of Belgium at Paris.
Mr Bliss Minister of U. S. A. at Stockholm.

Lord Derby.
Maréchal Lyautey.
Baron de Wedel, Minister of Norway at Paris.
M. Brunstrom, Consellor of Finland at Paris.
M. Lithander, Member of Parlement of Sweden.
Prince de Cystria de Faucigny Lucinge.
Duc Decazes.
Cherif Pacha.
Prince Radziwill.
Baron Robert de Rothschild.
Baron de Rothschild, of Vienna.
Comte Ch. de Noailles.
Prince Murat.
Comte de Cambacérès.
Comte Potocki.
Princesse Vlora.
Vicomte Neghib de Saab.
M. Anatole France, of the French Academy.
M. Francis de Croisset.
M. A. Fould.
M. Schneider, of Creusot.
M. Martell, of Cognac.
M. Rigaud, perfumer.
M. de Wendel.
M. Eric Cervin.
Madame Jeanne Lanvin.
M. Poiret.
Madame Paquin.
Mr. Mac Leen.
Sir Guy Standing.
Sir Arthur Levy.
Mr. Alex Gemmel.
Mr. Mac Kelvie.

Sir Roderick Wigan.
Mr. Lee.
Mrs Sofer Whitburn.
M. N. Prinsep.
Captain Wentworth.
Mr. E. Ashworth.
Mr. Vanderbilt.
Mr. Harriman of New-York.
Mr. Arnastad Peter, 3rd of New-York.
Mr. Richard Mac Creery of New-York.
Mr. Henry Plant of New-York.
Mr. Lorillard Ronalds.
Mr. Sol of New-York.
M. Louis Bréguet.
M. Nungesser.
M. Sadi Lecointe.
M. Cornuché, proprietor of the Casinos of Deauville and Cannes.
M. Letellier, Director of the news-paper " Le Journal ".
M. Bailby, Director of the newspaper " L'Intransigeant ".
M. P. Dupuy, Director of the newspaper " Le Petit Parisien ".
M. Durou, Director of the sports newspaper " Sporting ".
Madame Marguerite Lebaudy.
Mademoiselle Spinelly.
Mademoiselle Alice Delysia.
Mademoiselle Arlette Dorgère.
Mademoiselle Maguy Warna.
Miss Pearl White.
Mademoiselle Yvonne De Bray.
M. Sessue Hayakawa.
M. Rudolph Valentino.
M. Max Linder.
M. Dranem.

Large LABORATORY TYPE

ENGINE : 4 cylinder sleeve valve, monobloc. Bore 95 ⅜, stroke 140 ⅜. Special type. Magnesium pistons, special connecting rods. High pressure lubrication. Automatic carburettor. Tank under pressure or petrol pump. Special radiator. Ignition. 'Delco'. Electric starting off end of shaft by dynastart. . . . .
BODY CHASSIS : keelson supporting the whole of the members, engine, gear-box, springing, steering, set of accessories, gear-box forming block, 4 speeds forward and reverse on double sliding gear. Brakes on the four wheels. Oscillating back axle taking the torque, complete electric set, revolution counter, speed indicator, clock, thermometer, shock absorbers for the springs, complete outfit of tools, six wheels fitted with tyres, 4 seats facing forward. Speed on the level : 170 km. per hr. Petrol consumption : about 20 litres to the 100 kms. . . . .

23

---

there is very soon evidence that, in order to sell them, account was being taken of the social implications of ownership.

Comparatively ordinary cars like the solid British Armstrong Siddeley appeared in settings of magnificence only matched by the Hollywood musical at the height of its extravagance. This feeling was also very prevalent in the United States, where the houses of the great became ever greater, culminating in a series of advertisements for the Duesenberg – a car which probably deserved them more than any other – in which a series of male and female owners, each enjoying the rich life to the full, appeared with no other comment than simply 'He (or she) drives a Duesenberg'. The best of these anticipates, by nearly a decade, Orson Welles's *Citizen Kane* and shows the Duesenberg owner sitting in what can only be described as a house of cathedral proportions, while way up above him in the dim recesses is his wife, or for all we know his mistress, playing the organ. In antithesis to this, the Americans were also capable of simply showing how the ordinary car could

Even the eccentric Voisin sometimes conformed. 'When in doubt – list your Maharajahs.'

DUESENBERG

It is a monumental answer to wealthy America's
insistent demand for the best that modern engineering
and artistic ability can provide . . . . Equally it is a tribute to the
widely-recognized engineering genius of FRED S. DUESENBERG, *its designer,*
and to E. L. CORD, *its sponsor, for these men in one imaginative*
stroke have snatched from the far future an automobile which
is years ahead and therefore incomparably superior
to any other car which may be bought today.

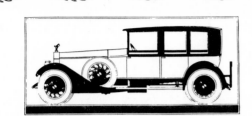

COACH work designed and built by Brewster & Co. was awarded a gold medal at the World's Exposition in Paris in 1878, and the *Legion d'Honneur* was conferred on the senior member of the firm. . . . American carriage makers celebrated the occasion with a banquet. . . . "In beauty, style and work-manship, I believe their carriages are unsurpassed," said the speaker of the evening, "but in one respect I take exception to them and I will state it confidentially to you gentlemen here, their carriages never wear out! I am like a boy with a toy; I like a new one now and then." . . . This statement, made about the famous Brewster carriages of fifty years ago, is even more impressively true of Brewster automobile coach work today. Indeed, it has been no uncommon thing for Brewster-built coach work to outlast two chassis; and cases are on record where it has been used on as many as five chassis. . . . The recent purchase of Brewster by Rolls-Royce places at the disposal of the American motorist a car unrivaled in beauty, staunchness, and riding comfort   a car with coach work as well as chassis to keep alive the tradition of "never wearing out." The illustration shows a Nottingham by Rolls-Royce and Brewster. Rolls-Royce Brewster, Fifth Avenue at 56th Street, New York. Also at all Rolls-Royce Branches.

ROLLS-ROYCE
BREWSTER

'Très snob – presque "cad" '
(with acknowledgements to *Punch*).

Overleaf: Park gates, noble piles, fountains, footmen and phoney crests; what more is needed to convince a man that he ought to buy a car? The Buick is 1921, the Cadillac 1926 and both, of course, are from General Motors.

85

THE NEW BUICK

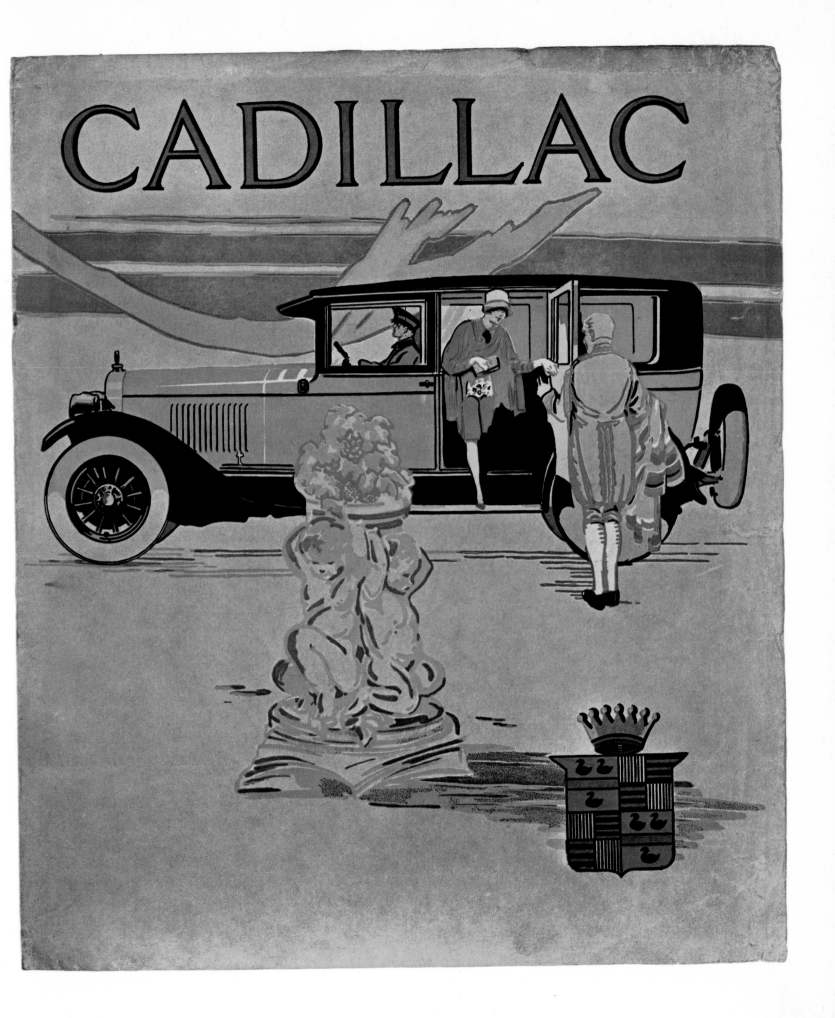

Chrysler arrived on the American scene late
(after the First World War) and when it came
to the European market was prepared to
throw tradition to the winds and let the new
young advertising designers of the day have
their head. Thus not only the cars but the
advertisements come as a breath of fresh
air.

Right: a catalogue cover, exploiting an early
use of printing on metallic papers in 1927.
This uses black and red on shiny silver and
was designed under Ashley Havinden's
direction by E. McKnight Kauffer.
Opposite: an 'inside spread' showing
Kauffer's clever use of the airbrush. Below:
Havinden's own design for a catalogue
cover in 1929.

Motorists in every civilised country have taken Chrysler to their hearts for its fine design, its perfect workmanship, its amazing comfort and its flashing performance.

Try a Chrysler for yourself on roads you know. Even the shortest run will tell you more about the enduring satisfaction of owning a Chrysler than anything we can print or paint.

All over Europe—from the white cities of the north—across the plains—through the mountain passes—to the sunshine of the tideless Mediterranean—Chrysler cars are carrying their owners, swiftly and smoothly, about their business or pleasure—and in almost every city along the great roads of Europe you will find Chrysler dealers always ready to help you.

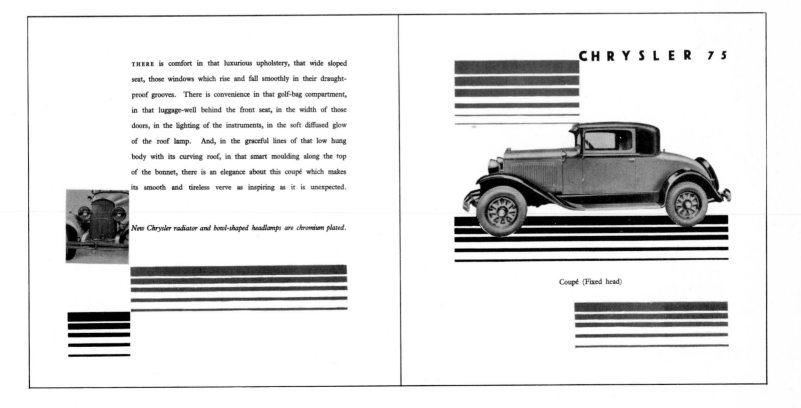

THERE is comfort in that luxurious upholstery, that wide sloped seat, those windows which rise and fall smoothly in their draught-proof grooves. There is convenience in that golf-bag compartment, in that luggage-well behind the front seat, in the width of those doors, in the lighting of the instruments, in the soft diffused glow of the roof lamp. And, in the graceful lines of that low hung body with its curving roof, in that smart moulding along the top of the bonnet, there is an elegance about this coupé which makes its smooth and tireless verve as inspiring as it is unexpected.

New Chrysler radiator and bowl-shaped headlamps are chromium plated.

CHRYSLER 75

Coupé (Fixed head)

ASHLEY

WE ARE COMING
IN THE CHRYSLER!

We shall not mind the rails and cobbles along the docks—(springs mounted in live rubber, shock absorbers, body built long and low—for steadiness!)

Out on to the great white road we shall shoot like a rocket— ('Silver Dome' engine, six cylinders, seven crankshaft bearings!)

Up, up the mountain side a hundred miles ahead we shall flash (crankcase ventilation keeping the engine cool and clean!)

Down again into the valley beyond we shall sweep, like a bird, without fear—(brakes hydraulic, self proportioning!)

We shall not be tired when we reach you.

We shall not be late.

We are coming in the Chrysler!

Three great 6-cylinder ranges—Chrysler Imperial 80, Chrysler 75, Chrysler 65! The four-cylinder Plymouth—also by Chrysler! Chrysler cars of every type and price. See the models in the dealers' showrooms.

WRITE FOR CATALOGUES · CHRYSLER MOTORS LTD · KEW GARDENS · SURREY

Two examples (reduced in size) of the Chrysler 'dream car' newspaper advertising campaign of 1929 (actual size: 15 in. across four columns). Other examples of this campaign, used throughout Europe, appear in the prologue to this book.

WE SHALL NOT BE TIRED WHEN WE MEET YOU WE SHALL NOT BE LATE!

Two hundred miles since morning. Two hundred miles to go. Four hundred miles of wet roads, rough roads, steep roads, narrow roads. Four hundred miles of sweet, safe, silent, exhilarating speed.

Our engine has six cylinders with seven-bearing counterweighted crankshaft — for smooth effortless power!

Our brakes are hydraulic, internal expanding—weather-proof, non-skidding!

Our springs are long—wide-set—anchored in blocks of live rubber to the frame!

WE ARE COMING IN THE CHRYSLER!

Three great 6-cylinder ranges—Chrysler Imperial 80, Chrysler 75, Chrysler 65! The four-cylinder Plymouth—also by Chrysler! Chrysler cars of every type and price. See the models in the dealers' showrooms to-day. Take the Chrysler of your choice on the road!

WRITE FOR CATALOGUES · CHRYSLER MOTORS LTD · KEW GARDENS · SURREY

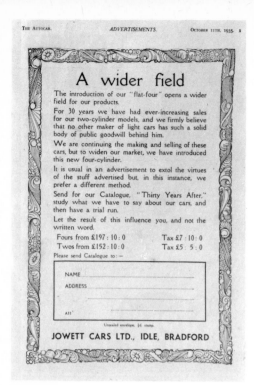

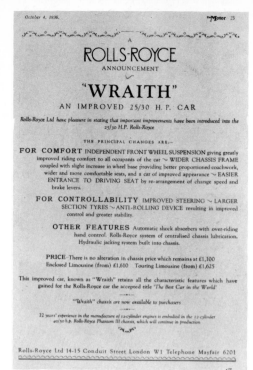

be an asset to the ordinary family. There were gay little scenes from everyday life, nowhere more charming than in the Chevrolet family who went for a picnic taking with them their own Boy Scout to light the fire.

Against these realistic and socially minded appeals can be found the often impressive abstract designs which range from Ashley Havinden's Chryslers in 1929 to the very flamboyant French efforts of a decade later where it is probably fair to suggest that the work of the coachbuilders on the cars themselves was in fact the influence behind the advertisement.

To be or not to be . . . In the mid-thirties pictures were suddenly 'out' and then just as suddenly 'in' and how slavishly they played follow my leader, from the rich man in his castle to the poor man at his gate. Incidentally the Jowett advertisement (top left) is one of a long series of 'copy' only advertisements that achieved considerable fame in their time.

The French, too, were in something of a rut but perhaps a more attractive one – the influence of Havinden can be all too easily traced.

Amid all this excitement there is also to be found, particularly in relation to the lower- and medium-priced cars, a much more straightforward effort to sell. A number of interesting slogans appeared and were widely used through whole series of advertisements. Perhaps the most easily remembered is one coined for the Austin Motor Co. 'You buy a car but you invest in an Austin'. Taken to its logical conclusion this kind of thing obviously carried great weight in terms of sales. Nowhere can it have meant more than in its ultimate sophistication as employed by the Packard Co. in America, who were quite

Solomon in all his glory was not arrayed
like this. These stoic Armstrong Siddeleys
of 1930 could hardly have been further
from the image they have here, which is
reminiscent of the Ziegfeld Follies.

'Ask the man who owns one'

This Hispano-Suiza catalogue of 1933 does
not need to rely on fairy-tale backgrounds,
and attempts to introduce the new typography.

The
IDEAL FAMILY
CAR
CHEVROLET

THE ENGLISH BUILT
CHEVROLET

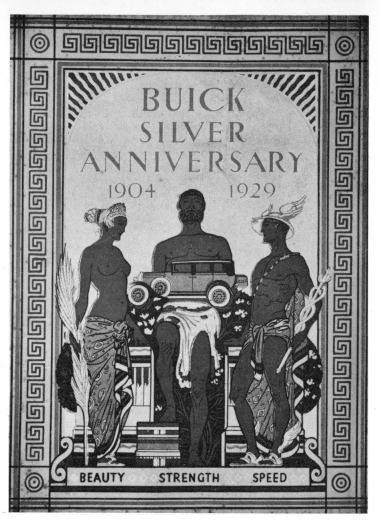

BUICK
SILVER
ANNIVERSARY
1904   1929

BEAUTY · STRENGTH · SPEED

Buick

THE CAR OF GREATEST ACHIEVEMENT

Ask the man who owns one

PAGE 97

1923 to 1939; and precious little to show for it. Always take a Boy Scout on your picnics (to light the fire). But the Germans, bottom right, come in with a terrific sense of style.

prepared not even to put the name of their product in the advertisement but simply to use their catchphrase 'Ask the man who owns one'.

Europe surprisingly enough seemed to take its lead from either America or Great Britain, and while Fiat were commissioning some important artists to do work for them a good deal of their advertising was run of the mill. The Germans, however, soon developed a style of their own and there is a kind of magnificent Teutonic splendour in many of the Mercedes advertisements, giving them both dignity and power, which still makes a staggering impact even today. Much the same might be said of any of the American advertisements in which the inside of the larger and more luxurious cars was brought very much to the fore. These are simply good photographs of comfortable interiors and they are still with us. They show comfort and luxury, taste and a sense of snobbery that has little need of copy to back it up.

Looking back over it now it seems a very curious mixture, a veritable curate's egg. Much of the design is exceedingly attractive by any standards, much of the work really good. Against this there is much very commonplace press advertising in which every square inch of the treasured space is filled, if not with copy, then with some announcement relevant or otherwise. And there is slavish copying all along the line.

THE STEP THAT ONLY PACKARD TAKES

'Ask the man who owns one'

These illustrations from a Packard catalogue are typical of a style which lasted throughout the thirties in America and which to some extent has influenced nearly all post-war car advertising.

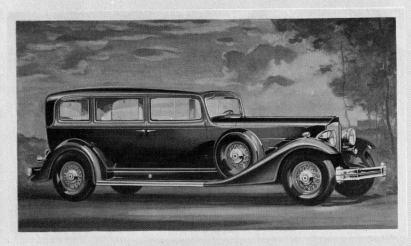

The PACKARD TWELVE SEDAN *for Seven Passengers*
As Executed in Inness Green

The PACKARD TWELVE LIMOUSINE *for Seven Passengers*
As Wrought in Titian Maroon

GEORGE INNESS was born at Kingston, N.Y., in 1825 and died in 1894. Abundant honors graced his painting life and he ranks as one of the American landscape painters generally known in Europe today.

The deep, luminous greens that characterize the art of Inness admirably fit this handsome motor car. It is shown against a background strongly reminiscent of *Afterglow*, one of his many medaled paintings.

TIZIANO VECELLIO, better known as Titian, was born in Cadore, Italy, in either 1477 or 1489 and died in 1576. He began his career at the age of eighteen, working in fresco, but in oils he reached his highest plane.

The glowing rich reds which have become legend through the deep shades in Titian's greatest pictures are well adapted to this big car that echoes the spirit of his palette and brush in its masterful coloring.

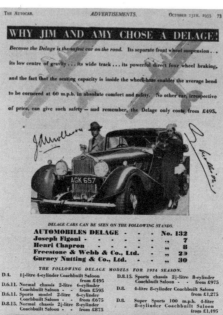

More Room
More Comfort

FROM DESIGNING THAT BEGINS WITH YOU

Basically, a motor car is a means of transportation. But so is a sleigh or a carriage or a horse. The difference (aside from speed) is that on the way to your destination, in a motor car, you should ride in utmost comfort. ❡ To accomplish that for you (and it is not a small task, when some of America's mountain roads are considered) Lincoln engineers plotted and charted carefully. They determined dimensions that permitted you to stretch out legs, and your head to clear the roof. This year, there is more room for you than ever in the Lincoln-Zephyr. ❡ Designers thought also of those who ride with you. Families may be smaller than a generation ago, but there are always the welcomed friends and guests. This car holds six without crowding (in the Sedan)—three up front, three in the rear.

Luggage space is greater than ever before. ❡ The Lincoln-Zephyr has always had an exceptionally wide windshield. But this year windshield visibility is increased 15%. There are actually 104 more square inches of glass in this front window. Winding roads in the distance, houses on the hills—all the world out front is spread before you! ❡ The Lincoln-Zephyr's "gliding ride" is an easy, forward movement—a gentle floating over road swells. Ribboned miles swing beneath the car. Villages appear on the horizon, and are soon left behind. Distance does not tire. ❡ This modern car was built for the open road. It has made its best records where demands upon it are greatest. The reason is that Lincoln-Zephyr designing begins with you. All the requirements of your journey have been anticipated before you start!

The Lincoln-Zephyr for 1940 is bigger inside than the car has ever been. Seats are wider, in front and rear. There is more room overhead, more around the feet, more shoulder room and elbow room. Six people ride in comfort—each has all the space required. The person next to the driver does not cramp him. There has always been plenty of space up front; there is more now, with the Finger-Tip Gearshift on the steering post. Journeys begin and end in comfort, with dispositions unchanged, when six travel the Lincoln-Zephyr way.

The good, the bad, and the indifferent. Chrysler have lost the Crawford touch and Auto Union are not Mercedes. Jaguar is on the way up but most agencies seem more intent in getting value for the space than in selling the value of the product. And above is the 'International Pin Head family' at work. The Lincoln Zephyr was not a small car; but it wasn't that big either!

Faced with so much from so many sources, it is impossible not to recognize how few styles and types predominate. We have the already mentioned and much in evidence country house, the setting better than the car. This was to become traditional and even now has not really left us. Here the elements of snobbism first appear, for although in some cases the cars are of the very top quality, in many they were comparatively cheap models and were quite unlikely ever to be seen in such settings or used by such people. Here, of course, is salesmanship; the family in their small saloon go for a picnic and all that can be seen apart from some small packets, which presumably contain sandwiches, are half-a-dozen bottles of champagne which in all honesty the family have not seen since their wedding. Arising from this attitude are those marvellous pin-head individuals who sit miniscule inside the smallest cars. They are of course 'artists' impressions' or else a special race of dwarfs must needs be born to take part in the studio sessions. There was the vogue for copy alone; and this aspect cannot be passed without reference to Jowett, who led the way for many years with their 'copy only' advertisements, surrounded by their neat printer's border; the sadness is that when the rest of the world moved away from the 'copy only' style, and reintroduced the photograph as a necessity, Jowett had to follow suit.

Towards the end of the period the Americans enjoyed a tremendous vogue in which could be found, month by month in the pages of *Fortune* magazine, carefully washed azure blue backgrounds ending in nothing more and nothing less than a great yellow Packard or what have you at the bottom of the page. Whether this technique sold cars or not is open to question, but it is unlikely that the Americans would have pursued it unless they were convinced of its worth. Equally stylish though quite different in technique were the French advertisements of the same period where design was everything, sometimes

Form" — gibt das Recht, bei diesem Wagen über die reine Technik hinausgehend von einem echten „Kunstwerk" zu sprechen. Die Daimler-Benz-Werke verfügen als älteste Automobilfabrik der Welt naturgemäß über einen einzigartigen Erfahrungsschatz, der ständig durch die vielfache Beteiligung an internationalen Wettbewerben ergänzt wird. Eine Hauptrolle spielen dabei die internationalen Automobilrennen. — Was in diesen schwersten Zerreißproben bestanden hat — sei es Material oder Konstruktion —, muß gut, ja es muß „das Beste" schlechthin sein. Ein ungeheures Maß an Können, Fingerspitzengefühl und feinstem Einfühlungsvermögen gehört aber dazu, dieses Beste auszuwerten und umzuformen für den Personenwagenbau. Um so dankbarer aber ist die Aufgabe für den Konstrukteur, wenn er rückhaltlos und ohne unbedingten Zwang zu möglichst niederer Preisgestaltung alle Erkenntnisse auswerten und das wirklich Vollendete schaffen darf. So ist es nicht verwunderlich, wenn wir beim „Großen Mercedes" mancherlei Merkmale antreffen, die wir an den jüngsten Schöpfungen der Mercedes-Benz-Rennwagenkonstrukteure bewunderten. — Bereits beim Fahrgestell beginnt die Parallele. Der Rahmen weist fast den gleichen Gesamtaufbau auf wie die Mercedes-Benz-Rennwagen, und besteht genau wie sie aus ovalen Stahlrohren. Nur die Dimensionen sind entsprechend größer und wuchtiger gehalten. Auf Grund der Rennwagen-Erfahrungen wurden auch die vordere Schwingachse und die Mercedes-Benz-Parallelradachse konstruiert, deren Wirkungsweise in dem Abschnitt „Interessante Technik" auf den letzten Seiten dieser Druckschrift

näher erläutert wird. Ein Wagen von den Leistungen und Abmessungen des „Großen Mercedes" erfordert ein besonders starkes, allen Bodenverhältnissen genauestens anpaßbares Getriebe. Ein 5-Gang-Getriebe, das vom 2. bis 5. Gang synchronisiert ist, wird allen Wünschen gerecht. Der starke 8-Zylinder-Reihenmotor ist durch das gut abgestufte Getriebe allen Erfordernissen der Straße in vollendetem Maße anzupassen. Die Maschine, die einen Hubraum von 7,7 Liter hat, leistet ohne Zuschaltung des Gebläses 155 PS. Bei Betätigung des Kompressors jedoch kann die Effektivleistung sogar auf 230 PS gesteigert werden. Die Spitzengeschwindigkeit liegt bei 170 gestoppten km/std. Vor Betrachtung der einzelnen Modelle auf den folgenden Seiten — serienmäßig stehen vier Aufbauten zur Verfügung — sei betont, daß allen Wünschen nach Sonderausstattung und Sonderaufbauten in weitestem Maße Rechnung getragen werden kann. Daß alles getan ist, um den Insassen des „Großen Mercedes" jede Bequemlichkeit und jeden Fahrkomfort zu sichern, versteht sich von selbst. Ein Hochleistungs-Radio-Apparat mit zwei Lautsprechern — die im Fond und im Armaturenbrett eingebaut werden können — schafft Abwechslung und Unterhaltung auf langen Fahrten. Große Kofferräume, breite Türentaschen und geräumige Behälter im Wageninnern sorgen dafür, daß großes Gepäck und die vielen während der Fahrt benötigten Reiseutensilien mitgeführt werden können, ohne die Insassen zu stören. In allen Modellen ist eine Warmluftheizung vorgesehen, die gleichzeitig die Windschutzscheibe beheizt und somit eine elektrische Scheibenheizung erspart. Die nächsten Seiten zeigen die vier Standard-Typen des „Großen Mercedes" und erläutern ihre besonderen Merkmale.

Die Pullman-Limousine des „Großen Mercedes" zeichnet sich durch eine vollendet schöne Linienführung aus, die dem Wagen trotz seiner außerordentlich wuchtigen Dimensionen ein elegantes und ausgeglichenes Aussehen verleiht. Im Wageninnern sind außer den für 2—3 Personen berechneten Fondsitzen drei große Klappsessel eingebaut, so daß in diesem Aufbau zusammen mit den Führersitzen Platz für 7—8 Personen vorhanden ist. Alle Sitze — auch die geteilt herausnehmbaren Vordersitze — sind den Körperformen glücklich angepaßt und schließen daher auch bei langen, sonst anstrengenden Reisen Ermüdungserscheinungen aus. Der Außenkoffer am Heck des Wagens dient zur Aufnahme von drei serienmäßig mitgelieferten eleganten Koffern von den Ausmaßen 830×500×230 mm, 830×500×230 mm und 930×650×200 mm (als Schrank). Für den gut entstörten empfangsstarken Radioapparat, der auf Wunsch eingebaut werden

kann, ist je ein dynamischer Lautsprecher unterhalb des Armaturenbrettes bzw. in diesem selbst und, soweit erforderlich, auch in der Trennwand zwischen Führer- und Fondsitzen vorgesehen. Die Einstellung erfolgt durch Fernantrieb vom Führersitz aus. Die Antenne ist im Dach des Wagens unsichtbar untergebracht. Die Belüftung ist zugfrei durch Glasblenden vor den herunterkurbelbaren Seitenfenstern. Sämtliche Fenster sind aus Sicherheitsglas. Durch einen Teleskop-Aussteller kann die Windschutzscheibe nach vorn geöffnet und in jede beliebige Lage verstellt werden. Die beiden Reserveräder sind seitlich in farbigen Metallhüllen untergebracht. Die elegant aussehenden Scheibenräder sind mit einer Bereifung von 8,25-17 versehen. Zur serienmäßigen Ausrüstung des Wagens gehören u. a.: Vollständige elektrische Ausrüstung mit Kotflügellampen, Nebellicht, Doppelscheibenwischer, eingebaute Fahrtrichtungsanzeiger mit Kontrolllampe, Aschenbecher mit Zigarrenanzünder über dem Armaturenbrett und je einer in den beiden seitlichen Armlehnen der Fondsitze, Kartenleselampe, Signalring auf dem Lenkrad, Fußabblendung, Innen-, Trittbrett- und transparente Nummernschildbeleuchtung, Rückblickspiegel, Zeituhren im Instrumentenbrett und in der Trennwand, Haltetaue an den Fondsäulen, Manteltau unter den Edelholz-Fächern, breite Türtaschen, vier große Handschuhkästen, reichhaltiges Werkzeug mit Vigot-Wagenheber.

PULLMAN-LIMOUSINE

Page 102

A leaf taken out of the American book (pages 98, 99) but improved out of all measure – Mercedes 1938.

'Ask the man who owns one'

He drives a Duesenberg   *She drives a Duesenberg*

to the point where it was difficult to recognize whether the thing was a motor-car or not, and out of this we must single the Voisin advertisements (which actually belong to an earlier period) which were as individualistic as the cars themselves, and one strongly suspects were the work of the car's own designer. Here, too, is an interesting throwback to the previous period with a list of distinguished customers, and Voisin was not alone in this. When all else failed, it was always a worth-while trick to list your maharajahs.

And as a postscript to this section, with a look at things to come, we find at long last sex reared its lovely head.

The understatement of the year . . . and anticipating Citizen Kane by nearly a decade.

Maturity and obsolescence: 1945 and after

'The want of the thing is perplexing enough, but the possession of it is intolerable.'
SIR JOHN VANBRUGH

For the second time in twenty-five years, motor manufacturers of the world found themselves recovering from a major war and facing the return to commercial life with a product which closely resembled the one they had been offering immediately before the commencement of hostilities. On this occasion the technical development of the motor-cars themselves during the war period was much less marked, but in production methods, and the kind of thing that went on inside the factories, a real development had taken place; and if the results of this development were not immediately evident to the public, they were certainly to have enormous impact on motoring over the ensuing years.

After the First World War the tragedy, in Europe at all events, had been principally one of loss of life; and the recovery of the participating nations (except for those which had been defeated) was not essentially an economic one. On the second occasion, however, it was soon seen that the economic wilderness that had been created almost throughout the world was in reality the major problem facing rehabilitation; and although the United States with its vast resources had fared better than most, the problems of rebuilding the world were to affect even the American economy, and indeed have so affected it that even today world monetary chaos remains.

In the immediate post-war period America was virtually unable to export to Europe since no one could afford to buy her products, while conversely it was essential for Europe to export to all countries of the world, including America, if survival was to be maintained. The most immediate and interesting outcome of this situation from the point of view of this book was brought about by American servicemen who remained in Europe after the war was over, where they discovered, to their intense delight, the existence of the sports car. This and all that went with it, its competition and its place in society, they took back to America, only pausing on the way to knock the second 's' off the name so that it became on their side of the Atlantic a 'sport car'.

It did not take long after the war before a spate of new models was thrust upon the public. The London Motor Show was revived in October 1948 and most of the 1949 models shown there were, in fact, new in some respect. The current range of American cars although not generally available on the British market was nevertheless to be seen in the exhibition and once more a comparison between what was happening in America and what was happening in Europe became possible. The most obvious difference was one of appearance, not so much in terms of size, for this has always remained a constant difference, but in general appearance. Most of the new British and European models retained at least some vestige of the mudguard or wing or as the Americans would have it the fender, whereas the current offerings from the United States had already dispensed with this and were beginning to become flat sided. It is true that on the English market, the new Standard Vanguard, which had been deeply researched at the command of Sir John Black, and to some extent the new Rootes models, were moving in the American direction. British Ford, however, at first contented themselves with the 'Pilot' which was only a reworking of the pre-war 22 h.p. British V8. The most interesting introduction in 1948 was probably the Morris Minor designed by Alec Issigonis and destined to stay in production with only very minor modifications for more than twenty years. Also at the 1948 Show was the new sports Jaguar complete with its XK engine which has had a similar life span; and while the Americans remained visually well in advance of the Europeans and were fast developing their automatic gear-boxes, most of the cars still employed the large old-fashioned side-valve engines which were already becoming obsolescent in Europe.

There were a number of births and deaths to be recorded in the early years after the war. Saddest of all was the disappearance of the big, 'grand' cars of French manufacture. For a short while after the war Delage and Delahaye continued in being, and there was in fact a post-war Bugatti although this never came to anything. Greater probably than either of these which were already beginning to suffer financial difficulties, were the products of the French Talbot concern, where Anthony Lago had taken over and was making exotic motor-cars which would have been entirely in place in 1938, and yet, having been further developed technically, were still infinitely desirable. For a while, too, a number of the great French coachbuilders survived, notably Saoutchik, and the old-established firm of Henri Chapron. Suddenly the French authorities decided that opulence must end, and crippling taxes wiped out an entire market of the world's motor industry in one sweep of a pen. Against this a new coachbuilding industry was to arise. The Italians, quickly recovering from the disasters of war, had cheap labour available in plenty and skill to go with it, both of which are prerequisites for the building of custom bodies, and firms such as Farina, Ghia, Bertone, and Michelotti were soon to become household names. They were further to develop their skills by offering designs to the major manufacturers of the world, even finding buyers within the purlieus of the United States. Not long after this the British coachbuilding industry almost totally disappeared, leaving only a combination of James Young, Mulliner and Park Ward (as a subsidiary of Rolls-Royce), who before very long were to remain the only real custom-builders of limousine class vehicles in the United Kingdom. Both Austin and Daimler hung on precariously for a while, and the latter may yet reassert its own individuality under the new banner of the British Leyland Motor Corporation.

By the middle of the 1950's a remarkable sameness was beginning to demonstrate itself, not only in the American industry and the British industry as self-contained entities, but even looking at the entire production of the world's motor-cars as one thing. Overhead valves, automatic gear-boxes, power-assisted steering, slab sides – the creation of what became known as the 'three-box' car (that is to say a box for the engine, a box for the passengers and a box for the boxes) – independent suspension, radial tyres, disc brakes, and all the things we nowadays expect to find on any car, became what they are, commonplace.

As the big cars became smaller, so did the small cars become bigger, and with the notable exception of Issigonis's second great essay, the Mini, almost every small car in serious production gradually grew and grew. Within fifteen years of the cessation of hostilities, the European motor industry was moving rapidly to cars of between 1000 c.c. and 3000 c.c. and ten years later than that, which is today, one can see that even this margin is being further reduced and we shall be working between 1500 c.c. and 2500 c.c., eventually perhaps to achieve a car for Europe of two litres capacity.

On the other side of the Atlantic a very different scene presents itself, for although the European sports car had been accepted and taken home as a kind of trophy of war to be enjoyed in one's own back garden, the small European car never really appealed despite the magnificent effort and comparatively high sales of the revived Volkswagen. It is an interesting sideline that this extraordinary little beetle, designed by Ferdinand Porsche for Adolf Hitler in 1935 and turned down by the British Control Commission in the period immediately after the war as having no commercial prospects whatever, should subsequently become perhaps the world's most widely known vehicle aided greatly by its clever advertising. But for all this and for all the success of the small European sports car in the United States, the American population turned resolutely against smaller cars.

Frightened by the threat of competition from Europe, most of the American manufacturers have at some time or other made forays into the world of the smaller car, known to them as 'compacts'. These, though far from compact by European standards, were diminutive by American standards, they were cheap and they were produced as competition for the several European saloons which were beginning to have some success in that market. However, within a year or two of their introduction the compacts became larger, and larger still, until they ceased to be compact altogether and practically ceased to exist.

We must also look at a recent development in the United States, pioneered by Ford with the introduction of the Mustang, and now followed up by most of the other manufacturers. Here a smallish, extremely high-powered car of sporting and European demeanour (available with a fantastic number of optional extras) is beginning to sweep a certain section of the American market. So successful has this essay been that Ford, with the new Capri, produced in both Britain and Germany, is now seeking to achieve a similar result in Europe.

The admission, then, has now been made. The door of the design department is now open to the sales manager and the 'ad man'; and the clean sheet of paper with which we might hope any designer would start his morning's work is already besmirched with the grey shadows left there by the requirements of the men who are going to sell his treasure.

But a certain number of treasures still do exist, and in a shrinking world where mass media and mass production have produced mass taste, there is still, strange as it may seem, a function in terms of luxury. This situation is perhaps most dramatically expressed by the decision of the Bugatti Owners Club – a club devoted to the preservation and adulation of one of the most individual and eclectic *marques* ever to be produced – to incorporate within its membership those owning Ferraris. In this upper sports field there are a number of manufacturers, principally in Italy, but also in Great Britain and Germany. And certainly the more exotic variations on the previously mentioned Mustang-Camaro type of American car must also be included.

Although in the two previous historical essays no particular account has been taken of the motor-racing and motor-sporting scene, it cannot pass altogether unheeded. From sporting and almost entirely amateur beginnings, motor-racing passed through a period of shadowy and insubstantial works support, into a period in the late 1930's when the whole business of motor-racing became a vehicle for the demonstration of national prestige. The resurgence of motor sport shortly after the Second World War quickly developed into a kind of circus of extreme commerciality, and although few of the racing cars which today appear on the circuits are in fact manufactured by a firm which also sells cars to the public, they are nevertheless most of them connected in one way or the other with major industrial effort in the world of motoring. The prestige which Ford have achieved with their Grand Prix engine or the remarkable effect, in terms of international marketing, of the long and continued series of successes in International Rallies by the British Motor Corporation's Mini-Coopers is almost incalculable. Oil, tyres, and other components are dragged into the scene, and what may once have been a sport is now little more than a spectacle – or, if you like, a circus in the best Roman sense. There is no room for regret in such situations; and, apart from the effect it may have in terms of sales and advertising, little to remark upon here. Indeed the situation was probably best summed up (and dismissed) in one sentence: 'Once it was gentlemen pretending to be mechanics, and now it's just mechanics pretending to be gentlemen.'

Lastly there are the industrial developments. When the motor-car first came into being innumerable manufacturers sprang up all over the world to make it. By 1930 most of the insignificant and inefficient had already disappeared, and the remainder were beginning to band themselves into groups. By the time the economic difficulties of the Second World War were really beginning to make themselves felt, big mergers were the order of the day, and as we now look at it there are, in fact, only four manufacturers in the United States: General Motors, Ford, Chrysler, and, coming a very small fourth, American Motors. These American interests have already spread throughout the world so that General Motors own Vauxhall in Great Britain and Opel in Germany. Ford have their own organization in Great Britain and another organization in Germany. Chrysler control Rootes in Great Britain and Simca in France, and who next swallows whom is anybody's guess. One firm alone in Europe has stood out consistently against this arrangement and that is Fiat in Italy, who have been making strenuous efforts to acquire some of the lesser companies. And in England the inevitable has happened. The great British Leyland Corporation has come into being and exactly where that starts is not so easy to remember. Originally Lord Nuffield (the manufacturer of Morris cars) absorbed into his modest empire Wolseley, Riley, and MG (the latter having always been part of it). This produced what was once known as the Nuffield Organization which ran in England parallel in size and power with Austins. Then came the beginning of the merger, Austin, Morris and Jaguar joining to become the British Motor Corporation. Starting from quite a separate base, British Leyland, one of the country's major producers of commercial vehicles who had already absorbed all sorts of other manufacturers in its own field, suddenly acquired Standard Triumph. On the sidelines of this deal the Rover Company acquired the Alvis Company and merged with Standard Triumph. The final merger was to bring the Leyland, Standard Triumph, Rover Alvis group under the same roof as Austin, Morris, Wolseley, MG, Riley and Jaguar. We are told that survival has dictated these moves, but it is the very question of survival which we must now face.

Against the development of these vast corporations a new range of specialist cars began to appear, many of them from small factories content to make a reasonable profit out of producing cars different from the mass. Not all of these were from the smaller firms, and a few outstanding examples, such as the forward-looking Citroën with its unique suspension and a body design which managed not to date in the course of more than twelve years, show that there was a social kudos in the production of the unusual. It remains to be seen if such ventures as the NSU, RO80 with its Wankel 'rotor' engine will succeed where engineering rather than appearance is the basis of a pioneer design.

Once upon a time to move about the world a man must walk or ride his horse or go in his own small carriage. From this private carriage the stagecoach began to provide public transport: then suddenly a man of genius gave us the railway so that all and sundry could sit in comparative comfort while one man did the driving. Afterwards came the motor-car, and within fifty years everyman had once again become his own engine driver.

The very freedom that the motor-car first brought and for which it was so much in demand is beginning to be its own executioner. Already in Belgium over 46% of the families in that land own a car of their own, and the French figure, surprisingly, is marginally higher. In Great Britain each and every motorist has only eight yards of road on which to run his car before he meets his neighbour. Sales and production soar and the motor-car is not yet one hundred years old. It seems most unlikely that it can ever see even its 150th birthday in the form in which we presently know it. Its use must surely soon be totally restricted or the whole concept of its design changed. In terms of history it will be very short-lived.

'Would you let your daughter marry a Ford owner?'

Looking at the last period in this book, one thing is very easy, and that is to forget how long a period it is that we are here dealing with. For most of those who were old enough to be part of, or to remember vividly, the Second World War it still seems to have happened only yesterday; and yet, in fact, the period since it ended is already longer than the period between the two wars. It must be accepted from this that a great deal has happened not only in terms of motor-car design, but in terms of advertising and social life; and little about this period is therefore likely to be representative of the whole. In fact the greatest change of all seems to have taken place during this time.

Just after the war the cars were pretty horrid, and one might say the same of most of the advertisements, although mercifully as always there will be exceptions. There was a good deal of harking back, a certain amount of plagiarism of what had been pre-war ideas, the most entertaining of which is undoubtedly Jaguar's decision to use the expression 'Pace, Grace, Space' when in fact in the period immediately before the war, the MG Car Company had themselves used 'For space, for grace, for pace'. It would be too trite to say that there was not over much of any of those commodities immediately evident, for in fact by the standards of their day, both the cars had more than a fair measure of the qualities claimed. Against this must be set the fact that it was more or less a seller's market, and most people were happy enough to be able to get hold of a new car at all. Indeed in Great Britain a covenant had to be entered into which made selling a new car once you had succeeded in getting one a more or less impossible proposition. In these circumstances it is little wonder that the advertisements were mostly concerned with bald statements of fact: there was little persuasion, hidden or otherwise.

This is also the period when the social implications of ownership come principally to the foreground. There is no denying that in the latter part of the 1930's there was some movement in this direction, but it achieved nothing by comparison with the effort of recent years, where the creation of the 'Jag belt', the fantastic sales of the Mercedes (which was much overpriced in Great Britain), and the introduction of numerous models from manufacturers using the word 'Executive' to imply that the owner was a cut above his next door neighbour, tell their own story. For the rest, in Europe generally there was a move away from the more traditional type of shape and interior furnishing, which was retained only in the more expensive and luxurious cars appealing to a more conservative public. For the new cars for the new people chromium

If you're the kind of a person who likes high-stepping action . . . then one of the fabulous '59 Buick Invicta models is the right car for you. For with just a touch of the accelerator Buick's new high-performing Wildcat 445 engine and fluid-smooth Twin Turbine transmission (both are standard equipment on all Invictas) whisk you out ahead with barely a whisper of effort. Try the Invicta two-door hardtop . . . and see what fun driving can really be!

INVICTA
THE MOST SPIRITED BUICK

1959 Buick Invicta two-door hardtop in Magic-Mirror Glacier Green

plate and jazz design of the worst conceivable kind enjoyed a veritable heyday and was also much in evidence in advertising. Across the Atlantic in the United States some of the shapes which appeared in the early fifties were more like nightmares than anything else, and provided numerous persons interested in psychology with endless opportunities to explain the deep sexual significance of these huge chromium protuberances and large red cavities which were all that were left to be seen as the great Behemoth disappeared into mid distance, on the road and, equally, on paper.

There was a great period of indecision and change, when the marketing world was for a time obsessed with detergent advertisements, each of them proving that something was whiter than something else. The appeal of the lowest common denominator was evident on all fronts and the motor-car and its advertising were not excluded. But as the market began to settle and as the financial considerations of present-day life began to bind the many small companies into the few big companies, so policy began to emerge, so style was imposed, and so, almost as the swing of a pendulum, we move once more from the blare of the trumpets to the sweet seductive strings of good typography and fine photographs. For if it is possible at so close a range to

1959: The introduction of people and events in a real rather than stereotyped way . . . 'if it's good enough for the movies it's good enough for you'.

'Would you let your daughter marry a Ford owner?'

new yorker deluxe FOUR-DOOR SEDAN

Neat but not gaudy – detail without disturbance (in 1954) and Mr and Mrs Jones rearing their ugly heads, demanding to be kept up with.

make such judgements it would appear that the 1960's is the age of the photographer; and also the age of group advertising. Examples of both these things appear in abundance in these pages. The many faces of Alfa Romeo only make a beginning; but the theme runs on until more recently the Rootes 'Myth Exploders' and the long series of both Volkswagen and BMC advertisements bring telling copy to bear on an existing series style.

Against this, and particularly from America, comes some of the most remarkable advertisement photography we are ever likely to see, and one cannot say that without some genuflection to the printers whose techniques have certainly kept up with the demands made upon them. The stately home with its attendant gates is still with us, and it is sad that almost the last advertisement by the Alvis Company before they went out of production, does not show British effort or British gates in a better light! Sex, although never very far away from many of the advertisements, is nevertheless strangely muted; and although the press day of every European Motor Show is rendered near intolerable by the bevies of largely undressed ladies sprawling about on the bonnets of motor-cars for the benefit of photographers, few of their efforts seem to be agency-inspired, so that the results are left to glorify

Chrysler | 1956

*Superbly styled
for the
Forward Look*

'Would you let your daughter marry a Ford owner?'

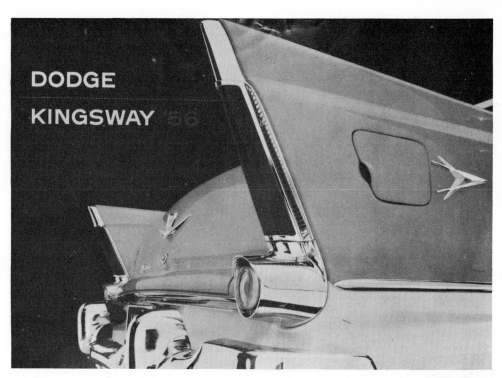

The increasing use of photography and the interest in detail, including the psychologist's delight – all those phallic rear ends.

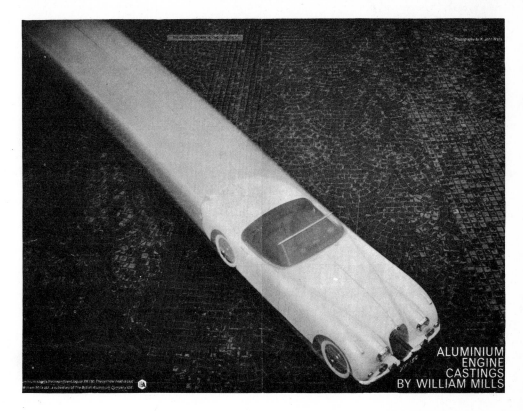

April 1962.

alfa romeo

By the end of the fifties the photographers were having a ball (and a very successful one), but only ten years earlier a selection of advertisements from the British motoring press makes one wonder why manufacturer paid the extra for colour. Students of design will find it hard to believe that the artist for the Daimler effort was Eric Frazer.

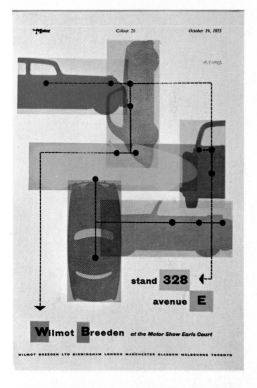

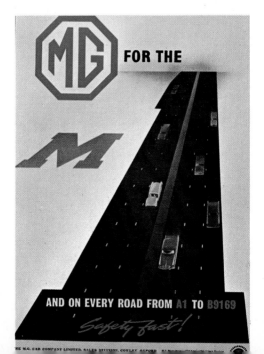

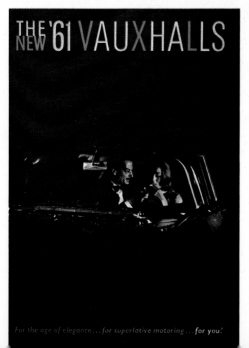

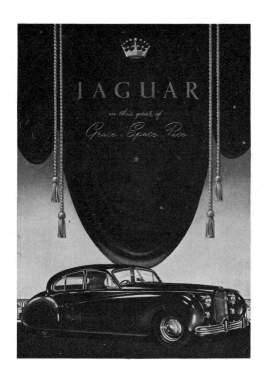

The long arm of coincidence. M.G. 1938:
'for space for grace for pace'; Jaguar,
fifteen years or so later: 'Grace Space Pace'.

L'Alfa Romeo 2000 Spider è una vettura Gran Turismo carrozzata dalla Touring, dedicata alla clientela che, nella produzione dell'Alfa Romeo, è solita apprezzare gli insuperabili caratteri delle sue tradizioni sportive. Derivata dalla 2000 berlina, essa ne possiede le caratteristiche meccaniche, esaltate da un motore di maggiore potenza e da una impareggiabile maneggevolezza conferita dal passo sensibilmente raccorciato.

'Would you let your daughter marry a Ford owner?'

The faces of Alfa-Romeo; not sex so much as allure and clever design.

Like pages from *Vogue*, the insidious charm
of the improbable made to look everyday.

'Would you let your daughter marry a Ford owner?'

CADILLAC CALAIS SERIES

ELECTRONICS
LABORATORIES INC

CALAIS COUPE

Today the bit that matters is the notice on
the right – the implication that electronic
engineers choose the Cadillac Calais Series –
but why, one wonders, Calais?

ALVIS
SERIES IV

Left: The last of the Palace Gate – an old idea getting steadily worse.

Right: But not the last of the Art Nouveau – an old idea getting steadily better.

only the editorial spaces. The winds of change are in the air and suddenly a comparison between the advertisements for motor-cars and those for furniture become rewarding and self-explanatory. Rakishness and speed sit on one side gazing stoically at low cost and reliability on the other, and yet if the truth be faced, most of the cars fit firmly in between the two.

For all the good design and for all the excellence of the new copy, an uncertainty is to be felt. Nobody seems to know quite what does in fact sell a motor-car, and most take refuge in the constant production of new models, the newness of which is open to some question from a mechanical standpoint, and the advantages of the new shapes are often not so clear when brought into everyday use. And just as one has had to ask what the true future of the motor-car is, after the first 100 years of its life, a similar question comes to mind in terms of advertising. Are the myths all exploded? Do the vague dreamlike figures sailing Walter Mitty-like in the azure blue backgrounds of

'Would you let your daughter marry a Ford owner?'

The Thunderbird Four-Door Landau

NOW...A LONG, SMOOTH, RICH, FAST FOUR-DOOR An historic, new Four-Door Landau . . . with full-width seating comfort for five . . . may be the most luxurious of all flying machines. Doors that swing wide, away from the center pillar, providing comfortable access to front and rear compartments. Stunning, exclusive Landau styling marked by its padded vinyl roof and gleaming "S" bars. New interiors styled for grace, dignity and unparalleled comfort. Relax in living-room refinement on specially sewn, tufted upholstery, available in luxuriant cloth, vinyl or distinctive leather, harmonizing with warm tones of simulated wood-grain appliques on instrument panel and doors, and deep, loop-pile carpeting. Sumptuous appointments. are found throughout the cockpit for matchless elegance that is synonymous with Thunderbird. Here's a bird that flies with impressive quiet whether powered by its mighty 390-cu. in. V-8 or a spectacular optional 428. Shift through the gears or go fully automatic, as the mood calls, with new SelectShift Cruise-O-Matic. Enjoy glorious wrap-around sound from a Stereo-Sonic Tape System or Thunderbird's new Multiplex Stereo Radio.

the new sports car really sell anything, or is the name and address of the local dealer set in some long forgotten type in the local paper all that we really need? Will we not soon go out and buy a car with the same lack of emotion with which we at present go out and purchase a new saucepan? Or is the converse true, that in a world getting forever more drab, this is the last bastion of personal excitement, the last flash left in our ever less exciting pan? – and in either case is anyone going to advertise the fact!

THE ACCENT'S ON ACTION!

A car doesn't really come alive until you turn the key to start the engine. This is the great moment in owning a Buick. With any one of Buick's six engines and four transmissions you've bought yourself a piece of action that just won't quit. And remember that along with its reputation for performance, Buick has been steadily building a reputation for economy—three winners out of four entries in the last Mobil Economy Run—the result of steady improvement in engine design and dramatic new automatic transmission efficiency.

Here's the line-up:

FIREBALL V6—a 225 cubic inch engine that turns up 155 h.p.♦ Smart performance. Great regular fuel economy. Available on Special, Special Deluxe and Skylark. Team it with Super Turbine (optional), regular 3-speed synchromesh or 4-speed synchromesh transmission (optional).

WILDCAT 445—One of the world's great performers. A 401 cubic inch V8 that scores 325 h.p.♦ Four-barrel carburetor. Regular equipment on Wildcat, Electra 225 and Riviera. Available with Super Turbine (standard on Electra 225 and Riviera) the regular 3-speed or 4-speed synchromesh transmissions (optional on Wildcat only).

WILDCAT 310—a 300 cubic inch V8 rated at 210 h.p.♦ A Mobil Economy Run winner with spirited performance. Available on Special, Special Deluxe, Skylark, regular equipment on Le Sabre & Skyroof Sportwagons. Goes with Super Turbine (optional), regular 3-speed synchromesh and 4-speed synchromesh(optional)transmissions.

WILDCAT 465—Performance and then some! A 425 cubic inch V8 that's rated at 340 h.p.♦ Four-barrel carburetor. Optional on Wildcat, Electra 225 and Riviera. Teamed with Super Turbine (optional on Wildcat, regular equipment on Electra 225 and Riviera) or 4-speed transmission (optional on Wildcat).

WILDCAT 355—300 cubic inches of get up and go that puts out 250 h.p.♦ This 4-barrel carburetor V8 is available on Special, Special Deluxe, Skylark, Sportwagons and Le Sabre. Goes with Super Turbine (optional) or with the regular 3-speed synchromesh or 4-speed synchromesh (optional) transmissions (except Le Sabre).

SUPER WILDCAT—Buick's mightiest V8! Twin four-barrel carburetors and a 425 cubic inch displacement give this magnificent engine a full 360 h.p.♦ Optional on Riviera, Electra 225, and Wildcat. Use with Super Turbine (optional on Wildcat, regular equipment on Electra 225 and Riviera) or 4-speed transmission (optional on Wildcat).

SPECIAL NOTE TO BOAT ENTHUSIASTS: Buick engines, V6 and 300 cubic inch and 401 cubic inch V8's, are now being modified for marine use by such engine manufacturers as Gray Marine, Outboard Marine, Universal Motor and Revley and are being currently used by boat makers like Sea-Ray, Matthews, Richardson and Trojan, further evidence of their outstanding durability. Consult your local boat dealer for details.
♦ *Released for export territories only where sufficiently high octane fuel is available.*

Once the power complex had engulfed the
United States the portrait of an engine
returned to fashion. What it tells it sells.

‘Would you let your daughter marry a Ford owner?’

**The 1966 Wildcat.
We checked out its tuning by driving it up and down steep mountain roads.**

We tested the new Wildcat very, very thoroughly. For instance, we drove down steep mountain sides; we tested the brakes, the engine, the body mounts, the frame, the suspension. The result? We give you a Wildcat for '66 that's tuned like a Swiss watch —every part works with every other part. On pavement, on dirt, on gravel, up hills and down hills, you'll never drive a tougher car —nor a more comfortable one.

Wildcat has a smart new grille this year. The front and rear views have been re-designed as well. Beautiful. Even the instrument panel inside is new.

Remember the mountain road bit? After that, we worked on Wildcat's suspension. And the frame. And the springs. And the stabilizer. We came up with a comfortable, but firm, ride.

In spite of the agile look, Wildcat is a big car— a family car. Take the wheelbase, for instance. It's 126 inches long. That gives you more family room inside. You could even pack in a tall dog. There's over 37 inches of head room in the rear.

We've got a new standard automatic transmission for the Wildcat this year, The Super Turbine— smooth, responsive power.

Pampering equipment. We've made available a whole closet-full of convenience features. Power steering, power brakes, AM-FM radio, bucket seats, reclining front passenger seat with head rests— the list goes on. Big car luxury never had it so complete.

Wildcat's standard engine this year is a 325-horsepower V8. More? Our 340-horsepower V8 is available.

There are four Wildcat models for 1966. A sport coupe, a 4-door hardtop, a 4-door sedan, and a convertible.

Have a ball at your Buick dealer's driving the 1966 Buick.

(Some of the equipment shown on the car illustrated is optional at extra cost.)

The Wildcat Sport Coupe

covers illustrated are a dealer installed accessory.)

Good ideas quickly go to seed when too often exposed: in 1966 you might expect better than those beastly little clouds of copy.

Here, particularly on the immediate left, is photographic style *par excellence*.

Corsair

First decide on a sporting saloon. Then select the version that matches your own style of driving. There are four models, V4 De Luxe, 2000 De Luxe, 2000E and 2000 Estate Car.

Rally Sport Camaro

FROM HIDEAWAY HEADLIGHTS TO UNIQUE TAILLIGHTS THIS CAMARO SAYS SWINGER FROM ALL ANGLES!

Specifying the Rally Sport Camaro really does electrifying things to the appearance. You get: "rs" emblems on the grille and going away on the fuel filler cap; full-width, black lattice grille with concealed headlights; lower body side molding; black accent below body side molding (with certain colors); color-keyed body accent stripes; sporty styling for parking/turning lights in front; sports-styled backup lights; and distinctive edged-in-black taillight treatment with two lamps in each

taillight unit for driving, braking and turn signal indication.

In addition to these outside eye-pleasers, you get bright metal front and rear wheel opening moldings, plus a bright drip gutter molding on sport coupes. Inside, an "rs" emblem appears on the steering wheel center.

What's the result when you're all through ordering your Rally Sport? You've fitted your Camaro with the action look that proclaims to all your exceptional trim selection.

Any of a host of power team combinations is available for your Rally Sport Camaro. You can have a Rally Sport Camaro with the standard 140-hp Turbo-Thrift 230 six-cylinder engine or 210-hp Turbo-Fire 327 standard V8. Specify another 327-cubic-inch V8 with a four-barrel carburetor and 275 hp if you like. The choice—and fun—is yours.

Personalizing your Camaro is one of life's more pleasant experiences. Check the list on pages 16-17 for items you can order; many items are also covered in text and illustrations throughout the catalog.

Open and shut case—concealed headlight system on Rally Sport Camaros. Grille sections blend when headlight is concealed for smooth, unbroken look.

Distinctive rear styling with twin-unit taillight assemblies edged in black, backup lights below bumper and "rs" emblem on fuel filler cap.

Rally Sport Camaro instrument panel in blue. Note "rs" emblem on horn button.

Rally Sport Camaro Convertible in Granada Gold.

While driving, it tells you about all the zip and comfort packed in it. In a small parking spot, it tells you why it's not bigger.

OLYMPIA will conquer your driving heart. We dare you to try it. You'll fall in love with it. It offers what you've only seen in big cars: Luxury. Sportiness. And it's a bargain. Because our opinion is that above-average comfort and quality should not be the privilege only of much more expensive cars. And it's your good right as a driver to choose a car that expresses your special wishes. One thing is certain. The OPEL OLYMPIA has — among many other features you'll soon get to know — the advantage of being a compact and handy automobile.

For young people, newlyweds, and the young in heart. You can see immediately that the OLYMPIA has no fancy gingerbread. Its looks are distinguished by crisp, clean lines and surfaces. Loads of snappy personality. A broad grille that integrates two headlight units. Smooth, beautifully proportioned sides. A sweeping, bigwindow fastback. Flowing down to 2 combination illuminators. They unify rear lights, stop-lights, direction blinkers, standard back-up lights.

2-door Sedan

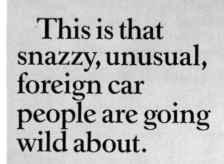

This is that snazzy, unusual, foreign car people are going wild about.

In France, Italy, Holland, South Africa, Denmark, etc, etc.

Those foreigners are a shrewd lot. They know a thing or two about motor cars.
That's why they choose British Fords: 200,000 of them last year.
More Cortinas are sold abroad than any other two British cars put together.
Out of every four cars we make, three

crafty foreigners snap up two of them.
And they're good payers. Last year Ford brought home £391 million in foreign currency. Not to mention the coffee, cotton, potatoes and toilet seats (yes, toilet seats) we got by bartering.
It's hardly a surprise we're Britain's biggest exporter.

We sell well abroad because they take our cars for what they are.
They don't go in for useless non-essentials like nostalgic radiator grills.
Or flashy statuettes. Or fancy badges.
They're realists.
They want a car to be a car.
And that's just what we give them.

Ford

As you can see from the chart we only came third at San Remo.
Still, to make up for it, we won the next 5 major International Rallies.
Which, though we say it ourselves, is quite an achievement for a car which is six months old this week. It's unheard of, in fact.

In the Scottish Rally we managed to beat nearly a hundred starters. Among them, the best cars in Europe.
This is probably an indication why the Escort is doing so well in the most important competition class of all.
The private car market.

Sorry about San Remo.

INTERNATIONAL RALLY SUCCESSES 1968				
Event	First Overall	Second Overall	Third Overall	Entries
1. San Remo Rally	Porsche 911T	Lancia Fulvia HF	Escort Twin Cam	72
2. Circuit of Ireland Rally	Escort Twin Cam	Mini-Cooper 'S'	Hillman Imp	122
3. Tulip Rally	Escort Twin Cam	Escort Twin Cam	Mini-Cooper 'S'	77
4. Austrian Alpine Rally	Escort Twin Cam	Lancia Fulvia HF	Renault Gordini	114
5. Acropolis Rally	Escort Twin Cam	Porsche 911L	Porsche 911T	56
6. Scottish Rally	Escort Twin Cam	Mini-Cooper 'S'	Hillman Imp	96

Ford

Frankness may frighten the board of directors but it sometimes appeals to the public.

Opposite: A collection of recent press advertisements which shows a welcome improvement on those of the mid-thirties (shown on page 100).

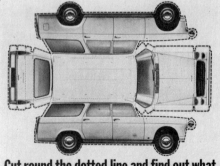

Would you let your daughter marry a Ford owner?

The Ford GT 40 £7540. 0-60 mph: 6 secs. 1st gear: 58 mph. Top gear: 164 mph. Boot space: laughable. Petrol consumption: wicked.   If you're a bit worried about your future son-in-law just ponder over the trade in value: 5 Escorts, plus 3 Cortina Estates, plus a Corsair 2000. You could become the first 9 car family in your road.

They say it's the red that makes beef so attractive.

'Would you let your daughter marry a Ford owner?'

BMC make the cars that hold the road.

e say a BMC frontwheel drive car holds the road better – come mud, snow, or hairpin bend. nd we're not handing you any line we can't keep.

BMC make the cars that fit where others can't.

A BMC transverse engine makes the car shorter outside, without losing inside. So you always get in everything – including the parking spots others have to pass by.

Overleaf: Making a virtue out of necessity – a reminder of the qualities the Joneses overlooked.

Slip into something hot this summer

Underneath the gleaming, polished paintwork lies a tough, all-steel body.

It's driven by a 1725cc engine with an aluminium cylinder head. With a 5-bearing crankshaft for smooth, quiet running.

It goes from 0 to 50 in under 10 seconds. And does up to 34 miles to the gallon.

It has an alternator instead of a dynamo. That makes the battery last longer.

18 cubic feet of luggage space.

It has a turn of speed up to 90 mph. And a turn of circle around 33½ feet.

Textured 'breathable' trim that takes any amount of sitting on. And reclining front seats.

You dial the ventilation, as and where you want it. And the stale air gets left behind, way behind.

There's a 2-speed heater boost. And 2-speed wipers.

£969 ex-works inc. P.T. (seat belts extra)

The beautiful, hot new Hunter is available for test driving at your local Rootes dealer. Go in and ask for the heat treatment.

HILLMAN   **Part of the new deal from Rootes**   HILLMAN  **ROOTES**

Parking is a lot of fun, especially afterwards
when you want to get the car out again, and
you find you've been left four inches in front
and five inches behind to play with,
and it's hot, and the sun has turned the car
into a Turkish bath, and you're working the
steering wheel one way, and then the other
and you're perspiring and turning the wheel,
and cursing and turning the wheel,
and crunch there goes a tail-light, then finally
you're out, and feeling just marvellous,
when a little old lady in a big new Zodiac
tries getting into your space, and she's
spinning the steering-wheel with one finger,
and for Pete's sake, she glides in in one go
and you wish you were dead.

The girl gets dated. The Triumph Herald doesn't

ANYTHING TO DECLARE ?

The Triumph Herald's bonnet opens wider than a suitcase—and just as easily

Following the strip cartoon and the TV soap opera the continuing theme finds new favour; all of them, incidentally, designed by Stanhope Shelton Mather and Crowther Ltd.

Only the Triumph Herald gives you four choices of coachwork
(and a fifth you can buy second-hand)

A dead end for other cars is a turning point for the Triumph Herald

The Triumph Herald is not just a pretty façade
—IT HAS A STEEL BACKBONE

The £642 Triumph Herald convertible lets the sun go to your head
(but not the skin)

Author's note

The decision to incorporate in this book a portfolio of advertisements from one single manufacturer stretching if possible from the earliest days of motoring up to the present time has always seemed worth while. The only possible difficulty might be one of choice. Quite a large number of manufacturers had to be considered in this context, since there are in every manufacturing country at least one or two companies which have been in the business from the beginning.

However, not all of them were able to provide a comprehensive record from their own files, and in many cases even the records of the Montagu Motor Car Museum at Beaulieu are incomplete; not all of them have continued in the same style of manufacture throughout the period; and many of them have changed hands or undergone reorganizations which make for differences of outlook during such a long period of time.

Nevertheless there are obviously several other manufacturers whose advertising would have served this purpose as well as that of Fiat. But since a choice had to be made, a choice has been made and is offered here without apology; but with acknowledgement that there are others equally worthy of consideration.

Seventy years of Fiat advertising: 1899-1969

Fiat was founded on 11 July 1899 and as with most other cars the first advertisement was probably only its nameplate, bearing simply the inscription 'Fabbrica Italiana di Automobili Torino', and it is from these initials that the word Fiat has come. The first car was a $3\frac{1}{2}$ h.p. model which was originally advertised in these words:
'Solidity, elegance, lightness. No worries, no noise, minimum consumption, prices which fear no competition, normal and de luxe bodywork, a vehicle for outings, for racing and for the mountains.'
Like most of the early cars this spindly affair had its engine underneath the seats and at the back, but by 1901 Fiat had produced its 8 h.p. model with the engine in what is now the conventional place and controls not dissimilar from those of a present-day motor-car. At this time Fiat took the step of interesting themselves in after-sales service, and a catalogue of that time reads:
'The company is always ready to give help in problems which may arise concerning the vehicle, and to put at the disposal of clients, where possible, skilled mechanics sending them also to clients' homes.'

By 1903 the car and the firm had grown further, and although that year's model did not have a nameplate on its radiator, there was a plate on the dash not far from the pedals in which the word 'Fiat' occurred for the first time, and with it the strangely shaped 'A' which was to remain part of the Fiat trade-mark until the present time. Although current advertising does not acknowledge this particular letter shape, it still appears on the badges of all the Fiat cars.

One of the most interesting things about the company has been the fact that almost throughout its life it has been concerned with producing ordinary, everyday cars for ordinary, everyday people, and although it has always been prepared to produce either a luxury model or a sports car of some distinction (and indeed at one time it produced racing cars of outstanding technical interest), it has always been with the everyday car that Fiat has been most preoccupied. Mass production commenced in 1919 with the model 501, which in many respects closely resembled the American car of that period, although it was a little smaller. An equal comparison might one supposes be made with the Morris Oxford. The Fiat 501 was designed by a lawyer, Carlo Cavalli, and something like 45,000 samples of it were made. A little less dictatorial than Ford, Fiat decreed that only the interior need be black; the exterior colours included dark blue, dark red, brown, maroon, dark grey, and green. If it can be accepted that man cannot live by bread alone, then obviously designers cannot live on mass production. As for copywriters, let the catalogue of the Super Fiat in 1922 speak for itself:

'After a life given over to work and study, the scientist, the artist, the poet, having reached maturity, has only one aspiration, to create his own masterpiece. To this ideal he dedicates whatever is best in him, passion, constancy and the most scrupulous care gazing on the monument which in one form or another will arise from himself with the sublimation of all his faculties. So Fiat, after a quarter of a century of life, intensely dedicated to perfecting every aspect of automobile construction, has created the Super Fiat; the sum of the aspirations of dedicated specialists of their experience, of their researches, of their most zealous attention, a most outstanding model, a mechanical achievement which is impeccable, the apotheosis of the motor-car.' And one might be tempted to hope the apotheosis of copywrit ing in the same breath!

1923 and 1924 saw more racing cars, and indeed Fiat went on making them until 1927. But in 1925 the introduction of the small 509 brought Fiat into that mass middle market where it has remained until today. By 1932 and the introduction of the 508 Ballila, the political movements in Italy were beginning to be felt. Mussolini had come to stay, and the really excellent Fiat advertising of the 1930's in no way dodged this issue. Many worthwhile artists were employed to produce a wide range of advertisements in which they quite evidently had a reasonably free hand. In contrast to this we find some rather curious 'modern' art of the late 1930's, some of which was not without hilarity. The blue lady striding towards her small Fiat appeared in fact in two guises. In the second version the cloak from her shoulders was longer, and designed to conceal her rather ample rump, for what we are now given to understand were religious reasons! But through the good and the bad, one thing remains, and seems always to have been a part of the Fiat approach; it is on the whole unemotional and unspectacular. It pays comparatively little service to the class distinctions of owning a motor-car, and treats it always as something to have and something to use. No doubt Fiat's almost unique position in being the only sizable motor manufacturer in the country, and certainly the only one making cars for the ordinary people, has had some bearing on this; and although some of the early advertisements had a splendidly colonial aspect, and some of the more recent ones play the

'Happy Families' game for all it's worth, the approach remains astonishingly consistent over a vast number of years.

In the period immediately after the last war, it does become a little messy, but without losing sight of its ultimate object. Then suddenly a fresh wind blows, a new and tremendous effort is made to achieve a coherent style throughout everything that is done; and yet it never loses the ordinary touch. The car is still a car, something to use, something to have. There is an interesting sidelight in that while most European manufacturers are busy hurrying off to the south of France and the coasts of Africa to get a 'suitable' atmosphere in which to photograph their motor-cars, Fiat set off for the cool, somewhat damp green spaces of Ireland, just to prove that a motor-car can be peaceful and useful, and need not necessarily be glamorous at all. As always these are ordinary cars for ordinary people. Walter Mitty can take his custom elsewhere.

The very boldness of most Fiat advertising is perhaps the secret of its success, as is its willingness to go with the feeling of the moment.

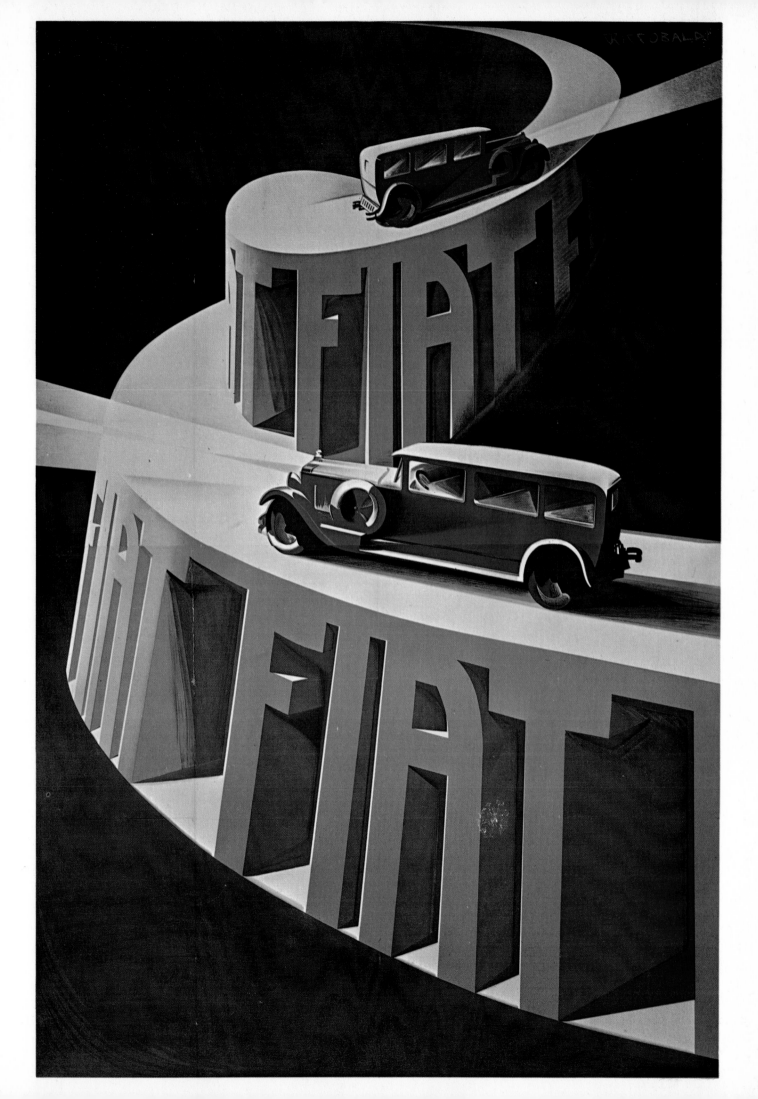

Fiat 8 HP and Fiat 12 HP with Count Biscaretti of Ruffia, President of Turin's Automobile Club, in Italy's first automobile tour 1901.

tice è a doppia estensione, di tela impermeabile, con linea completamente parallela alla scocca ed è munito di tendine laterali. ✻ La vettura è inoltre fornita dei seguenti accessori: un porta ruota laterale a destra, tre ripostigli sotto ai sedili ed ai fondi, un piccolo porta bagaglio posteriore con riparo per la scocca, due fari e tre fanali regolamentari elettrici e una fodera a sacco di tela nera per il mantice.

La vettura Torpedo

La vettura Modello 70 carrozzata Torpedo è capace di due posti anteriori uniti e di tre posti posteriori, coperti di pelle nera lavabile con guarnizioni a fascie e senza bottoni. ✻ La scocca è del tipo a linea completamente diritta e la sua parte anteriore forma corpo unico con il « coupe-vent » ed il cofano. ✻ I parafanghi sono in un sol pezzo, senza bulloni: quelli anteriori sono uniti allo chassis per mezzo di « bavettes » in lamiera. ✻ Le pedane sono di legno ricoperte in lincrusta e bordate di metallo. ✻ Alla parte anteriore dello chassis è applicato un « pare-brise » ad un solo cristallo, con colonnine per l'attacco del mantice. ✻ Le parti interne degli sportelli sono munite di borse di cuoio. ✻ Il pannello posto dietro ai posti anteriori è ricoperto in « moquette ». ✻ I fondi della carrozzeria sono ricoperti nella parte anteriore di lincrusta e nella parte posteriore con un tappeto in « moquette ». ✻ Il man-

[PAGINA 13]

[PAGINA 14]

'Lest you should think he never could recapture...' well Fiat could and did. An interesting sideline: the lady in the bottom corner later appeared with her cape extended to her knees; the Church having observed that her ample rump was a little much for 'good taste'.

In 1922 the Fiat 519 was announced in a manner that perhaps suggested it needed to be helped on its way by the Olympic figure in the background. The lorry opposite still has its wheels firmly on the ground, but manages to suggest rather more of its true character.

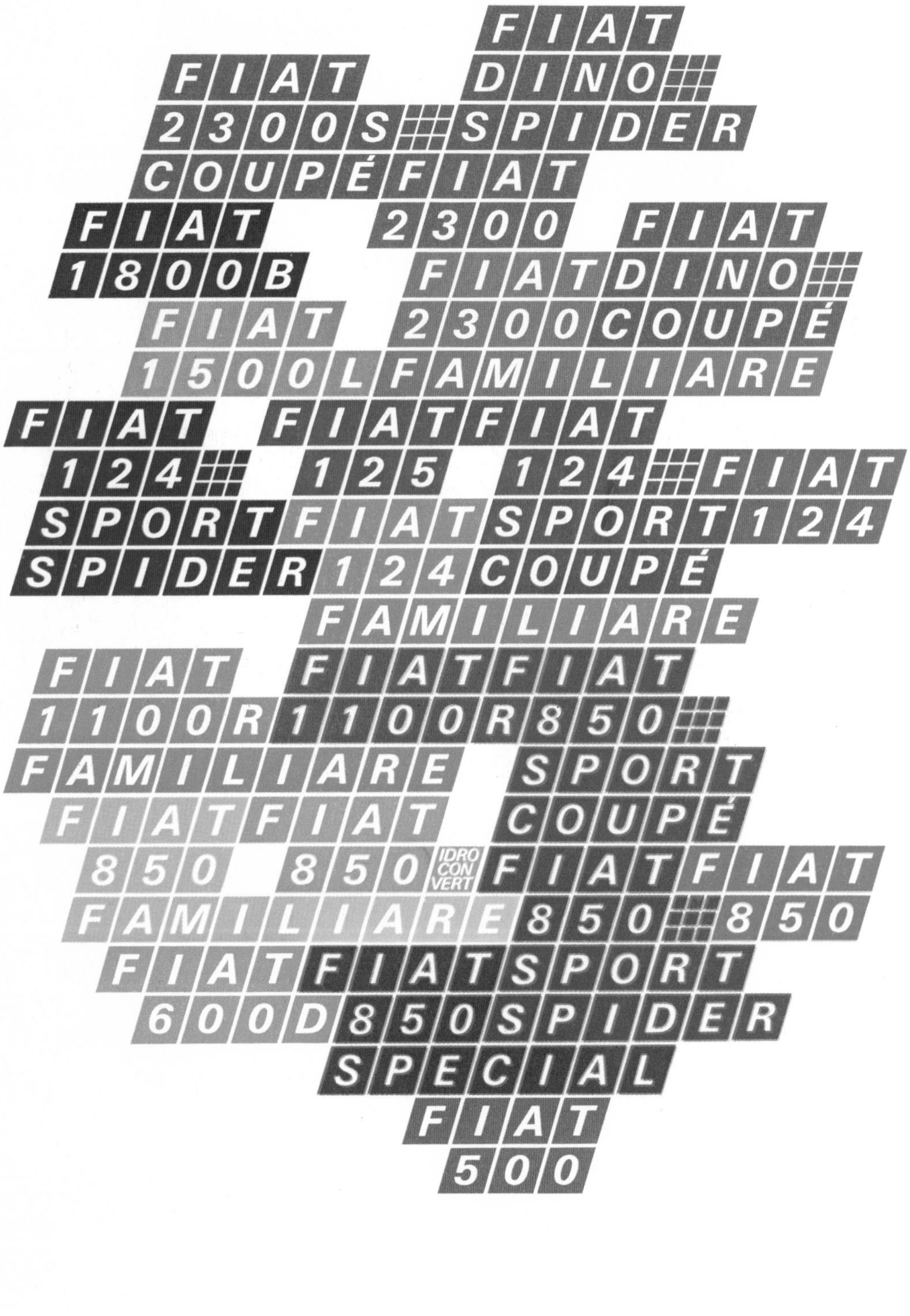

FIAT
FIAT DINO
2300S SPIDER
COUPÉFIAT
FIAT 2300 FIAT
1800B FIATDINO
FIAT 2300COUPÉ
1500LFAMILIARE
FIAT FIATFIAT
124 125 124 FIAT
SPORTFIATSPORT124
SPIDER124COUPÉ
FAMILIARE
FIAT FIATFIAT
1100R1100R850
FAMILIARE SPORT
FIATFIAT COUPÉ
850 850 IDRO CON VERT FIATFIAT
FAMILIARE850 850
FIATFIATSPORT
600D850SPIDER
SPECIAL
FIAT
500

The new broom – a system for advertising that now follows Fiat all over the world. It is a pity they did not keep the odd-shaped 'A', it would have helped identification.

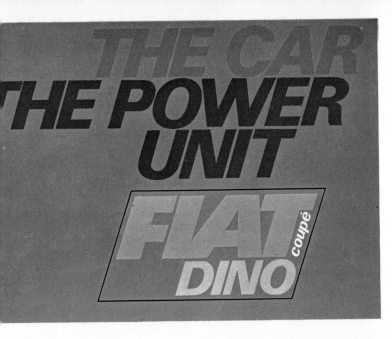

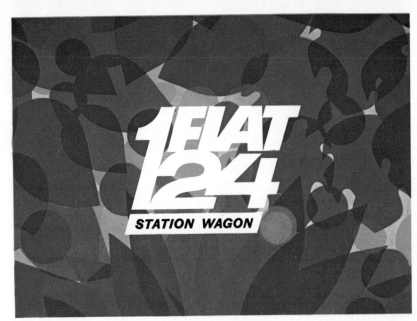

Affidatevi

alle piccole cilindrate Fiat
per la loro robustezza e sportività
per la loro economicità
e maneggevolezza
per la loro sicurezza

da 500 a 850 cm³
da 18 a 47 CV (DIN)
da 95 a 145 km/h
da 2 a 7 posti
500 berlina e giardiniera
600 D berlina
850 berlina
familiare, coupé, spider

FIAT 500
FIAT 600 D
FIAT 850

affidatevi alla Fiat
alla sua organizzazione di vendita e assistenza
in Milano, Filiale e Commissionarie

Affidatevi alla 124

per la sua modernità
per la sua robustezza
ampiezza e sicurezza
per la sua agilità e ripresa

60 CV (DIN)
oltre 140 km/ora
albero motore a 5 supporti
5 posti, 4 porte
bagagliaio 385 dm³
4 freni a disco
niente ingrassaggio
L. 1.035.000

FIAT 124

affidatevi alla Fiat
alla sua organizzazione di vendita e assistenza
in Milano, Filiale e Commissionarie

Affidatevi alle 124 Sport

per la loro sicurezza
per la loro potenza e bellezza
per la loro tenuta di strada
per il loro confort

1438 cm³
90 CV (DIN)
doppio albero a camme in testa
albero motore a 5 supporti
4 freni a disco
170 km/ora
124 Sport/spider (5 marce)
L. 1.550.000
124 Sport/coupé 4 posti
L. 1.490.000
(5ª marcia a richiesta
con supplemento di prezzo)

FIAT 124 SPORT COUPÉ
FIAT 124 SPORT SPIDER

affidatevi alla Fiat
alla sua organizzazione di vendita e assistenza
in Milano, Filiale e Commissionarie

Calco-liamo 124

60 CV (DIN)
oltre 140 km/ora
albero motore 5 supporti
5 posti
4 porte
bagagliaio 385 dm³
niente ingrassaggio
4 freni a disco
sicurezza, confort

L. 1.035.000

un calcolo attuale, interessante, conveniente FIAT 124

Nuovo motivo di successo Fiat al Salone di Parigi

Model				Model			
600	499,5 cmc.	18 CV.	~ 95 km/h	1500 L	1481 cmc.	75 CV.	145 km/h
600 D	767 cmc.	25 CV.	~ 110 km/h	125	1608 cmc.	90 CV.	160 km/h
850	843 cmc.	37 CV.	~ 125 km/h	1800 B	1795 cmc.	82 CV.	~ 145 km/h
850 Special	843 cmc.	47 CV.	135 km/h	2300	2279 cmc.	102 CV.	180 km/h
850 familiare	843 cmc.	34 CV.	> 100 km/h	2300 familiare	2279 cmc.	102 CV.	160 km/h
850 Sport coupé	903 cmc.	52 CV.	> 145 km/h	2300 S coupé	2279 cmc.	130 CV.	~ 190 km/h
850 Sport spider	903 cmc.	52 CV.	> 150 km/h	Fiat Dino coupé	1987 cmc.	160 CV.	~ 200 km/h
1100 R	1089 cmc.	48 CV.	> 130 km/h	Fiat Dino spider	1987 cmc.	160 CV.	~ 210 km/h
1100 R familiare	1089 cmc.	48 CV.	> 130 km/h				
124	1197 cmc.	60 CV.	> 140 km/h				
124 familiare	1197 cmc.	60 CV.	> 140 km/h	CV = DIN			
124 Sport coupé	1438 cmc.	90 CV.	> 170 km/h				
124 Sport spider	1438 cmc.	90 CV.	170 km/h				

Make your own puzzle – choose your own
car. No sex, no snobbery, just Fiats.

nuovo FIAT 616N2

51 Cv (DIN)
la potenza del nuovo motore

1650 kg - la portata conveniente
per molteplici impieghi

3500 kg - il peso totale
che consente la guida a tutti

su 3500 km
di autostrade
e strade italiane
decine e decine di

centri mobili di assistenza a tutti gli automobilisti.

Sono i furgoni
dell'assistenza vacanze.
Assistenza ACI-Fiat
su tutte le autostrade.
Assistenza Fiat
sulle strade
di grande traffico.*
Fanno servizio di giorno,
compresi i festivi,
su un tratto
di 50 km ciascuno.
Sono forniti di una speciale
dotazione di soccorso
e collegati via radio con
i centri fissi ACI.
Assistono, soccorrono,
riparano. (37000 interventi
nel 1967). Rendono
i viaggi delle vacanze
più sicuri e regolari.

giugno
luglio
agosto
settembre

FIAT

Assistenza vacanze

* Ponte S. Luigi - Savona / Livorno - La Spezia / Ravenna - Ancona
Brennero - Trento / Arona - Cannobio / Paola - Praia a Mare
Catania - Messina / Catania - Siracusa / S. Teresa di Gallura - Olbia

Get moving with Fiat
Fiat land
Fiat sea
Fiat air
Raw materials
are transformed
into means
for transport.
The past, the present
and the future
motivated
by the spirit
of scientific research.
Collaboration
in air space research.
Meanwhile the present
divides itself
to improving
and experimenting
for tomorrow:
Fiat nuclear energy.
Fiat steel production
and Fiat metallurgy.
For mobility,
number one: the cars.
At the measured pace
of our time.
From one country
to another.
From one town
to another.
From door to door.
Fiat trucks for transport:
heavy, medium
and light.
Fiat agricultural tractors
and earth movers.
For urban and
inter-urban transport:
Fiat buses.
Fiat marine engines
and gas turbines.
Fiat aviation.
Fiat rail rolling stock.
Fiat lubricants.
Fiat machine tools.
Factory spares
for millions of cars,
trucks and tractors
all over the world.
For a Fiat, Fiat service.
Move, travel
ten minutes,
one hour,
twenty-four hours
in the great comfort
of our time.

The return to typography – the language, like the platform, is 'immaterial'. Style speaks for itself.

Fiat in the United Kingdom: **FIAT**
Fiat (England) Ltd.
Northdale House, North Circular Road, London N.W. 10
Fiat Tractors Ltd. 35 Berkeley Square, London W. 1
Fiat S.p.A. 35 Berkeley Square, London W. 1

Again the magazine technique – but with
'heightened' photography. In the factory
even Fiat are prepared to add glamour – the
workers need it.

Officine di Rivalta:
produzione di
complessivi
meccanici e
carrozzerie, e
allestimenti di vetture
sportive o speciali.

Usines de Rivalta:
on y construit
les groupes
mécaniques et les
carrosseries pour
voitures sportives
et spéciales.

Rivalta Shops:
production of
mechanical
and bodywork
assemblies for
sports and
specialty cars.

Das Werk in Rivalta:
hier werden
mechanische
Baugruppen und
Karosserien
hergestellt sowie
Spezial- und
Sportwagen gebaut.

Talleres de Rivalta:
producción de
conjuntos mecá-
nicos y carrocerias,
montaje de coches
sport y especiales.

Dopo le linee
di lastroferratura
i moderni impianti
di verniciatura.

Après les chaînes
de tôlerie, voici
les installations
modernes de
peinture.

The body shell lines
and the modern
painting equipment.

Nach den
Blechbearbeitungs-
strassen, die
modernen
Lackieranlagen.

Después de las
cadenas de
chapistería
las modernas
instalaciones
de pintura.

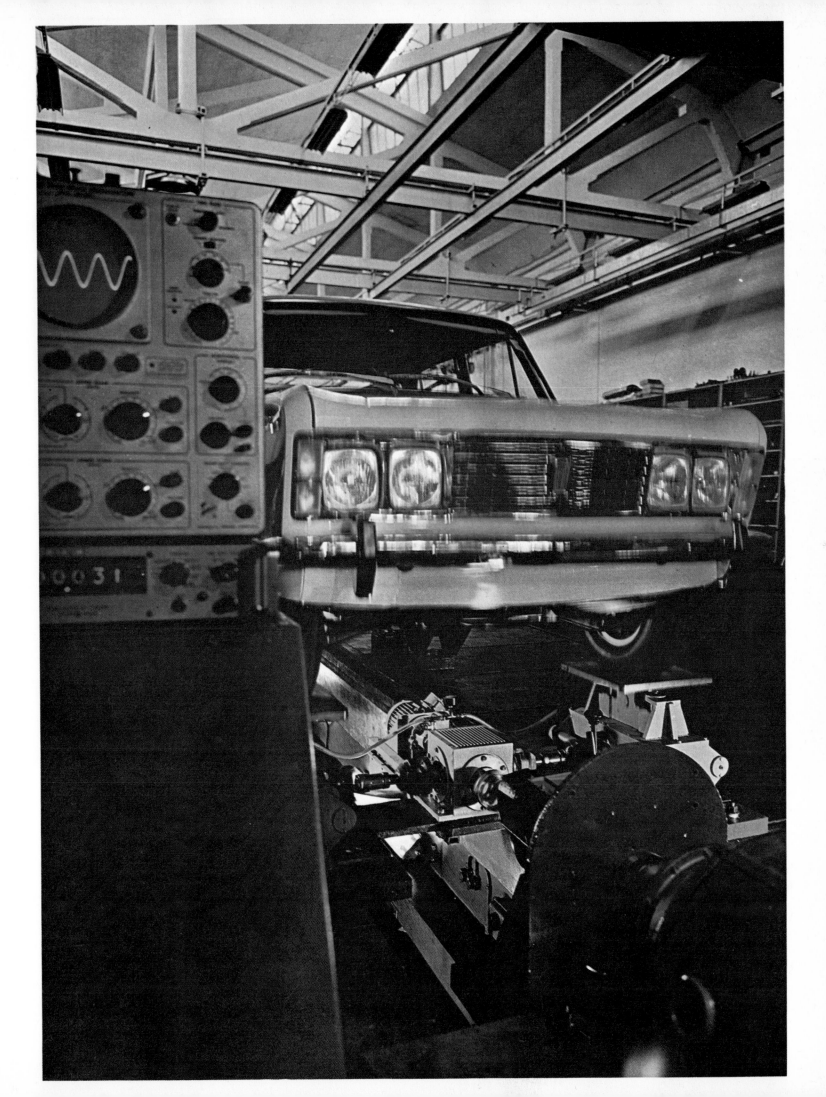

The cool, quiet approach. The antithesis of
Ford in Morocco, Vauxhall in the dust. Fiat
went to Ireland to take these pictures – and
were content to say 'It is only a car'.